BACKROAD BICYCLING
on Cape Cod, Martha's Vineyard, and Nantucket

25 Rides for Road and Mountain Bikes

Second Edition

Susan Milton and Kevin & Nan Jeffrey

BACKCOUNTRY Backcountry Guides
Woodstock · Vermont

Although it is unlikely that the roads you cycle on these tours will change much with time, some road signs, landmarks, and other items may. If you find that such changes have occurred on these routes, please let the publisher know so that corrections may be made in future editions. Other comments and suggestions are also welcome. Address all correspondence to:

Editor, Backroad Bicycle Tours
Backcountry Guides
P.O. Box 748
Woodstock, VT 05091

Library of Congress Cataloging-in-Publication Data

Milton, Susan, 1951–
Backroad bicycling on Cape Cod, Martha's Vineyard, and Nantucket : 25 tours for road and mountain bikes / Susan Milton and Kevin and Nan Jeffrey.—2nd ed.
       p. cm.
    Rev. ed. of: 25 bicycle tours on Cape Cod & the Islands. c1996.
    ISBN 0-88150-51-3 (alk. paper)
    1. Bicycle touring—Massachusetts—Cape Cod—Guidebooks. 2. Bicycle touring—Massachusetts—Nantucket Island—Guidebooks. 3. Bicycle touring—Massachusetts—Martha's Vineyard—Guidebooks. 4. Cape Cod (Mass.)—Guidebooks. 5. Nantucket Island (Mass.)—Guidebooks. 6. Martha's Vineyard (Mass.)—Guidebooks. I. Jeffrey, Kevin, 1954– II. Jeffrey, Nan, 1949– III. Milton, Susan, 1951– 25 bicycle tours on Cape Cod & the Islands
GV1045.5.M42 C366 2001
917.44'920444—dc21

                                                          00–068859

Cover design by Bodenweber Design
Text design by Sally Sherman
Cover photograph by © David Brownell
Maps by Inkspot: A Design Company, © The Countryman Press

Published by Backcountry Guides, a division of The Countryman Press,
   P.O. Box 748, Woodstock, Vermont 05091
Distributed by W. W. Norton & Company, Inc., 500 Fifth Avenue, New York, NY
   10110

Printed in the United States of America

10 9 8 7 6 5 4 3 2 1

Dedication

For Cynthia Eagar and Tim Coggeshall

Backroad Bicycling on Cape Cod, Martha's Vineyard, and Nantucket

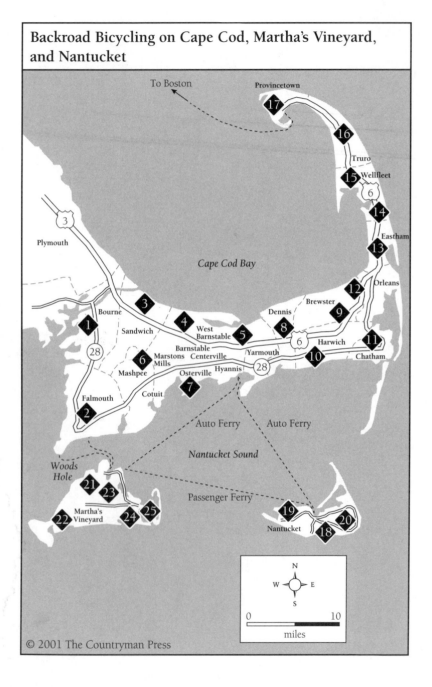

To Boston

Provincetown

17

16

Truro

15 Wellfleet

6

14

Eastham

13

Plymouth

3

Cape Cod Bay

12 Orleans

Brewster

9

Dennis

3

Bourne

4

West
Barnstable

5

8

Harwich

11

Sandwich

Barnstable

6

Yarmouth

Chatham

Marstons Centerville
Mills

6

Mashpee

Osterville

Hyannis

28

10

7

Cotuit

Falmouth

2

Auto Ferry   Auto Ferry

Nantucket Sound

Woods
Hole

21
23

Passenger Ferry

19

20

22 Martha's
Vineyard

24 25

18

Nantucket

N

W   E

S

0   10

miles

Contents

NANTUCKET

MARTHA'S VINEYARD

Preface to the Second Edition

This new edition was a chance to rediscover the Cape and the islands after five years of daily distractions. It's amazing what can change. A town changed its name. Two lighthouses moved. Towns bought land and created trails and new places to explore. Once-quiet roads are busier. Businesses changed hands and names.

For those reasons, there are many changes in these tours.

One tour leads to a new spur in the Cape Cod Rail Trail. Four other tours sample new off-road bicycle trails—actually, they lead riders to those trails. The adventure is up to you.

S.M.

Backroad Bicycle Tours at a Glance

Tour	Region	Distance (miles)
1 Bourne, North Falmouth, and the Cape Cod Canal	Upper Cape	18.2
2 Falmouth and Woods Hole	Upper Cape	26.4
3 Sandwich and the Cape Cod Canal	Upper Cape	18.6
4 West Barnstable and East Sandwich	Mid-Cape	17.8
5 Barnstable and Yarmouthport	Mid-Cape	12.6
6 Marstons Mills, Mashpee, and Cotuit	Mid-Cape	19.0
7 Centerville and Osterville	Mid-Cape	13.5
8 South Dennis to Chapin Beach	Mid-Cape	21.2
9 Brewster, Harwich, and Nickerson State Park	Lower Cape	20.7
10 South Dennis and Harwich	Lower Cape	18.3
11 Around Chatham	Lower Cape	17.3
12 Brewster, Orleans, and Eastham	Lower Cape	23.4
13 Around Eastham	Lower Cape	13.0
14 North Eastham and South Wellfleet	Lower Cape	21.0
15 Around Wellfleet	Lower Cape	23.5
16 Around Truro	Lower Cape	22.7
17 Provincetown and North Truro	Lower Cape	20.2
18. Around Nantucket Town and to Surfside	Nantucket	10.7
19 Nantucket Town to Madaket	Nantucket	19.3
20 Nantucket Town to Siasconset	Nantucket	21.3
21 Vineyard Haven to West Tisbury	Martha's Vineyard	19.3
22 West Tisbury, Chilmark, and Aquinnah	Martha's Vineyard	25.2/33.4
23 Vineyard Haven, Oak Bluffs, and Edgartown	Martha's Vineyard	18.0
24 Around Edgartown and to South Beach	Martha's Vineyard	10.4
25 Edgartown to Chappaquiddick	Martha's Vineyard	11.2

Terrain	Highlights
Flat to gently rolling	Scenic harbors, historic towns
Flat to gently rolling	Scientific port of call
Mostly flat, a few hills	Along the Cape Cod Canal
Mostly flat, a few long hills	Bump along village's cartpaths
Flat to gently rolling	Peaceful ride by early American homes
Mostly flat, some gently rolling	Mashpee River walking trail
Flat and sheltered	Villages with historic hearts
Flat, one incline; sheltered	Cottages of a summer playground
Moderate hills; mostly sheltered	Cranberry bogs; the state's oldest park
Flat; mostly sheltered	New rail trail by conservation areas
Hilly	Bay, beach, and ocean
Flat, with rolling hills	From park to beaches on a rail trail
Flat, some inclines	Old Cape Cod on quiet roads
Long inclines, exposed	Lighthouses and a national seashore
Hilly, some long inclines	Scenic ride by art galleries and beaches
Hilly and demanding	Golden landscapes of hills and valleys
Hilly on trails, flat on roads	The Pilgrims' first landing place
Flat with 2 moderate climbs	Homes of whalers and traders
Some challenging hills	The cartpaths and vistas of Sanford Farm
Flat to gently rolling	Easy ride to a jewel of a village
Flat	Rural woods and shady state forest
Long, exposed inclines	A thriving general store and sea cliffs
Mostly flat, some hills	Gingerbread cottages
Flat and sheltered	Beautifully preserved whaling village
Flat, partially exposed	Ferry ride to an island getaway

Introduction

The heritage of Cape Cod, Martha's Vineyard, and Nantucket is among the richest in the United States—Native Americans, Pilgrims, and Quakers; whaling and shipbuilding; Finnish farms and the Sandwich glassworks; cranberry bogs and fishing; the Kennedy compound and the Woods Hole Oceanographic Institution.

The fascinating history of these shores, however, cannot hold a candle to their beauty—to the long sweeps of beaches, the sea cliffs, the panoramas of bays and moors, the harbors and thickets of woods. Sights on these tours will sometimes take your breath away.

Long summer playgrounds, the Cape towns and the islands of Nantucket and Martha's Vineyard are the year-round home of many who fell in love with their character, got "sand in their shoes," and had to stay. What keeps these people here is part of what you'll discover bicycling this unique slice of New England.

Cape Cod looks like a flexed arm, reaching out 30 miles into the Atlantic Ocean from Massachusetts before curving north and then west toward the mainland. The Cape has three geographical areas: The Upper Cape, the western portion closest to Boston, includes the towns of Bourne, Falmouth, Mashpee, and Sandwich; the Mid-Cape area in the center includes the towns of Barnstable, Yarmouth, and Dennis; and the Lower Cape to the east includes the towns of Brewster, Harwich, Chatham, Orleans, Eastham, Wellfleet, Truro, and Provincetown. Part of the Lower Cape is often referred to as the Outer Cape, usually Wellfleet, Truro and Provincetown. Cape Cod is separated from the mainland by the Cape Cod Canal, itself crossed by an automobile bridge at Sagamore and an automobile bridge and railroad bridge at Bourne.

Nantucket—an island, a county, and a town—is 14 miles long and 3.5 miles wide and lies roughly 30 miles south of the Cape. Martha's Vineyard is 24 miles long and 10 miles wide and lies only 7 miles south of Cape Cod.

Cape Cod, Martha's Vineyard, and Nantucket were created by lobes of a glacier advancing and colliding over this area 25,000 years ago. On a return visit, the glacier created the moraines that run north to south on the Upper Cape and west to east along the Cape's northern shore.

Melting ice later washed sediments into plains around the islands and the Cape, while the rising sea level made the high elevations into islands and the arm of the Cape.

Since then, wind and water have shaped the glacial deposits, eroding cliffs to create barrier beaches and islands, moving sand to close bays and shores, and then breaking through the land again to change shorelines and habitats.

The first settlers of the Cape and two islands were members of the Wampanoag nation. More than 30 tribes and even more subtribes inhabited these shores, and their early presence is reflected in the names of places, especially villages, such as Nauset, Skaket, Pamet, Madaket, Nobscusset, Sippewisset, Quisset, and Pocasset. The first Native Americans were likely nomads with seasonal camps on bay shores in the summer and fall and inland camps in the winter.

Cape Cod and the islands became one of the first places that intrepid European explorers stumbled across. The Vikings may or may not have camped on the Cape, but we know that early visitors included Florentine explorer Giovanni da Verrazano exploring for Spain in 1524, Bartholomew Gosnold for the English in 1602, and Samuel de Champlain for the French in 1605. The Cape was a busy place even before the Pilgrims sailed into Provincetown Harbor in November 1620.

Cape Cod is named after the fish, which was plentiful here when 16th-century explorers sailed into these waters. Whaling, lobstering, fishing for cod or haddock, scratching for quahogs, cultivating oysters—this region's history has long been tied to its fisheries, with their cycles of plenty and scarcity.

Profits from fishing and trade during the Civil War helped to build many of the elegant houses you'll see as you tour around Cape Cod and the Islands. Whaling and fishing voyages led to trade, which led to the building of clipper ships that set records for Atlantic crossings under sail.

Seafarers from these waters traveled the world and brought cosmopolitan views and experience back to their native towns and islands. Now a visitor must search for a restaurant or market that sells locally caught or raised fish. Fishing fleets are mostly idle due to dwindling fish stocks that experts say need 10 to 15 years to rebuild. Cape and Island towns are trying to diversify by promoting aquaculture or by farming oysters, lobsters, and quahogs in tidal lands and bays. In the colorful harbors of Provincetown, Nantucket, Hyannis, Chatham, and

Susan Milton

One of the Cape's inviting beaches in Wellfleet

Sandwich, working fishing boats are still present among the charter yachts and private boats.

Native Americans taught colonists about cranberries, which grew naturally in the sandy soil of the Cape and the islands and were valued for their nutritional and medicinal properties. All over the Cape and Islands you can see the flat bogs surrounded by drainage ditches where cranberries are cultivated today. In the spring, the bogs are surrounded by the hives of bees that pollinate the vines. In autumn, the bogs turn a brilliant crimson as the berries ripen. Many of the tours described in this book take you past working cranberry bogs.

Overwhelmingly white and Protestant, the Cape and Islands gradually attracted other pilgrims in search of a better life, people who all left traces of their cultures in the industries, food, and churches here.

By the late 1890s, Finns from factory towns in Massachusetts were moving to Cape Cod in search of outdoor work, creating a small settlement in West Barnstable. Like the Finns, Cape Verdeans were highly regarded for their cranberry work and developed a strong farming and fishing economy in Harwich and Falmouth. Portuguese from the Azores first arrived on Martha's Vineyard aboard whaling vessels, settling in such ports as Provincetown and maintaining strong ties with their island homes. (Today, kale soup is as common as clam chowder in local restaurants, and barbecues may feature linguica as well as hamburgers and hot dogs.) African blacks and escaped slaves signed on to work on ships and in shipyards on Nantucket. The Cape and Islands offered stops on the Underground Railroad supported by Quakers and abolitionists.

The first Irish immigrants arrived to work in the glass and other factories in Sandwich in 1825. Both Irish and Italians helped to build Cape Cod's canal, its bridges, and many of its resort hotels, and they stayed on to live here. In recent years, workers from Brazil are adding to the Cape's year-round population, along with summer workers from Ireland and Jamaica.

Today, much of the Cape's special atmosphere is created by the accessibility of beaches for walking, fishing, and swimming. The 27,000-acre Cape Cod National Seashore, created in 1961 over strong local opposition (now replaced by pride), stretches from Provincetown into Chatham and attracts close to 5 million visitors annually. As you bicycle along preserved back roads, past long-existing houses or cottage colonies, following the tours described in this book, you will witness the difference that the park has made in preserving the Cape.

In recent years, each Cape and Island town has devoted money to buying open space, preventing pollution of coastal waters, and regulating development. To buy land, each town draws on a land bank financed by a 3 percent surtax on real estate or land transfers. Martha's Vineyard and Cape Cod have special commissions that, with varying degrees of success, try to plan and channel growth in existing towns and preserve the Cape's environment. The goal of these efforts is to preserve the distinct identity of the Cape and the islands without preventing their residents from adapting to modern times. "There may be no use in being overly nostalgic about a nonreturnable past," naturalist John Hay wrote in his introduction to a history of Brewster. "But there is a great deal of point in recognizing the value of the place you live in, and that certainly includes its history, human and natural."

The Roads

Most of the primary roads on Cape Cod and the islands replaced Native American footpaths and colonial cartpaths. Small wonder that, until the

1900s, most travelers came by sea rather than attempting to arrive by coach over the wandering roads that ran through towns and harbors and to landings.

The construction of Route 6 (the Mid-Cape Highway) in the 1950s made Cape towns more accessible from the mainland and spurred a development boom. The highway, built on the high glacial moraine along the Cape's spine, connects with county roads to historic Route 6A on the north side and Route 28 on the south side. Those state roads still clog in the summer and, regrettably, are still impossible to avoid for any length of time. The tours in this book frequently cross, or—when absolutely necessary—travel along these roads for short stretches.

Because of the Cape's tourist season, major road repairs are banned between Memorial Day and Labor Day. This means they are frequent in the spring and fall.

The road-sign system is simple and most intersections are well marked. Town roads usually carry descriptive or directional names. The only confusing signs are on Route 28 on the Lower Cape. The signs say 28 north or 28 south rather than the proper east or west; highway engineers seem unable to acknowledge that the road follows the curve in the Cape.

Many Cape and Island roads are charming and scenic, but narrow and winding. They require caution, especially for children, families, or groups.

The national drive to turn abandoned railbeds into bicycle trails, with no fees, is well represented on Cape Cod and the islands. The railroad built in the early 1880s was abandoned on the Lower Cape by 1965 and bought by the state for a rail trail in 1978. The popular Cape Cod Rail Trail covers 25 miles between Route 134 in Dennis and LeCount Hollow in Wellfleet. The paved trail requires frequent crossings of roads. Bicyclists are asked to dismount and walk across. There are plans to extend the trail into Yarmouth and to create a new spur from the trail into Chatham.

In Falmouth, the Shining Sea Trail offers a scenic 4.0-mile-long route from Locust and Mill Roads in Falmouth to Railroad Avenue in Woods Hole. Two other popular bike paths parallel each side of the Cape Cod Canal, along canal service roads. The north-side trail is 6.5 miles long, and the south-side is 7.7.

On Martha's Vineyard, bike trails connect Oak Bluffs (along State

Beach) to Edgartown and beyond to South Beach, with a return loop inland between Edgartown and Vineyard Haven. There are other paved trails through the state forest. Nantucket has five major bike trails, from Nantucket Center to Siasconset and back, to Madaket, to Dionis Beach, and to Surfside Beach.

All trails are shared by bicyclists, pedestrians, in-line skaters, and, on the Cape Cod Rail Trail, horseback riders. Other local bike trails double as sidewalks in many Cape and Island towns; many such trails are part of these tours.

In recognition of growing bicycle traffic, many towns are defining bike lanes, between white lines and road shoulders, along neighborhood roads. Under Massachusetts law, riding on sidewalks through business districts is banned, but this ban is rarely enforced, except on the islands, where police will ticket offenders. Growing friction between pedestrians and discourteous bicyclists may prompt Cape towns to follow suit to prevent more collisions and near-misses.

Weather and Seasons

The bicycling season in this part of Massachusetts runs at least from late April to November, with spur-of-the-moment trips possible the rest of the year during bouts of great weather.

The busiest time on the Cape and the islands is July and August, the prime beach-vacation time, especially for families. But, in recent years, weekenders are drawn from early May to late November by chowder suppers, crafts fairs, farmers' markets, auctions, and yard sales.

Many year-round residents take their vacations in September and October, when beaches and roads are quiet, restaurants and shops are still open but uncrowded, and the weather is warmer and less fickle than in spring.

Take your choice: glorious thaws in January sometimes permit shorts and sunbathing. In April, May, and June, lengthening days bring the bright blooms of daffodils, lilacs, beach peas, and lady's slippers. Temperatures may zoom to the 70s or, during April blizzards, plummet to the teens. In July and August, daytime temperatures rise into the 80s and muggy 90s, but with the prevailing sea breeze the Cape and the islands are usually cooler than inland areas of Massachusetts. On the hottest days, early-morning or late-afternoon rides are refreshing. Between

Susan Milton

Deceptively steep trails meander through beach plums and scrub pines on Race Point in Provincetown

September and November, daytime temperatures fall from the 70s to the 50s; to the 60s by Halloween. You will ride along leaf-strewn roads, past hedgerows of purple asters, goldenrod, and beach plums, and catch sight of migrating flocks of ducks and geese. The Cape's autumnal display, starting in late September and peaking in mid- to late October, is muted but not to be missed.

Remember, coastal weather is changeable and unpredictable. Do not let poor weather or a sour forecast ground you. Rain in Truro may mean sunny skies over Orleans because of the way squall lines travel only over parts of the Cape or Islands. Before canceling a day's tour, call a place on your route for an on-the-scene report.

Choosing the Right Tour for You

After checking the weather report, consider the distance, terrain, and exposure to wind. The Cape and the Islands are known for their wind-whipped beaches and shore roads, exhilarating but tiring. Although reputed to be flat, Cape Cod does have a few gradual inclines and some hills that will send you searching for your lowest gear.

A 20- to 25-mile ride will be agreeable to a beginning rider or occasional exerciser. Beginners may join biking or tour groups that sponsor tours, complete with support wagons and leaders.

Thirty to 40 miles a day is comfortable for an intermediate cyclist or regular exerciser, with time to spare for lunch, beaches, and shopping. None of our tours is for longer distances, although due to the close proximity of the tours in this book you may want to link two or more together.

Since each geographic area on the Cape and the islands has a distinct physical beauty all its own, you will probably want to sample them all. Beginning with the Upper Cape and Mid-Cape areas, you will find large inland tracts of white pine and scrub oak forests dotted with deep, sparkling ponds and a large concentration of working cranberry bogs. Heading toward the Lower Cape, coastal areas gradually shift from the confinement of Cape Cod Bay to the north, Buzzards Bay to the west, and Vineyard and Nantucket Sounds to the south, to the wilder exposures of the Atlantic Ocean. Beyond Orleans, the land narrows and flattens into a region of shifting sand dunes and wind-stunted trees, vast marshes and frequent glimpses of the sea.

Martha's Vineyard seems to be a physical composite of Cape Cod's landscapes, from the sea-swept, fog-enshrouded cliffs of Aquinnah to the woods and farms of West Tisbury. Nantucket possesses that almost mystical physical quality of all small islands far removed from the mainland, as though its very existence is a gift from the sea.

Using the Maps and Directions

Begin by reading each tour's introduction to find a tour that matches your available time, energy, interests, and mood. A blustery day may not be a good day for a short ride interrupted by sunbathing, but such a day will still be good for wave-watching. Look at the map for a general sense of the route.

All directions are printed in bold at each mileage point. They usually refer to obvious landmarks such as town-line markers, railroads, and intersections to orient you and to prevent you from total reliance on a bicycle computer.

We regret that we could not list all points of interest on or near these tours. You may wish to check a detailed map of Cape Cod and the islands if you like to improvise. You may also wish to read about the Cape and

Islands before your visit. Suggested maps and books are listed in the Resources section, below.

The restaurants and other dining places mentioned in descriptions are often local landmarks, places that we recommend to friends, and, in most cases, open year-round—an important feature in this seasonal economy. More complete lists of lodging places and restaurants are available from local chambers of commerce.

Selecting Your Bike

The tours in this book may be enjoyed on a touring bike, a hybrid or cross-bike, or even a mountain bike. All of the rides feature paved roads, with several stretches along dirt roads.

We do, however, recommend 1.125-inch or wider tires on touring bikes to see you safely across stretches of sand and soft shoulders. We also recommend that a hybrid or cross-bicycle be equipped with 1.375-inch tires, which work well on any surface.

Other Considerations

- Carry a jacket; coastal weather is unpredictable, especially in the spring and fall. It's perceptibly cooler near the shore, even in summer, and rain showers may douse you when you least expect it. For a comfortable, even enjoyable ride in the rain, wear breathable rain gear. The moisture can't soak through, but your perspiration can escape. Inexpensive vinyl or rain-resistant jackets work for short, occasional rides. Avoid ponchos, which tear easily and catch wind like a sail. During the spring and fall, you may want to carry tight-fitting thermal pants and a headband or cap that can be worn under your helmet.
- Wear a helmet. Fortunately, helmets are increasingly light and comfortable to wear. Be sure to choose a helmet that states it meets Snell and ANSI safety specifications. A well-fitting, properly adjusted helmet should sit evenly on your head without tilting back.
- Unfortunately, we must recommend a bicycle lock if you plan to stop for any length of time. Lock your bike frame and wheels to an immovable object.

- A rearview mirror is useful to prevent you from veering out into traffic as you look back over your shoulder. There are models that snap onto helmets, handlebars, or brake hoods.
- Bicycle computers make it easy to follow the written directions and determine your speed. These small devices clip onto your handlebars and record your mileage (in miles or kilometers), speed, current time and date, average speed, and total distance covered. It's a fascinating device, but don't let it distract you from the scenery.
- Cyclists with sore feet or ankles may choose to wear cycling shoes with an extra-firm sole. Padded cycling gloves help prevent sore palms, elbows, and shoulders, and can help cushion a fall.
- A good pair of sunglasses will protect your eyes from the glare of the sun and water, as well as from flying insects, dirt, pollen in June, and other airborne debris.
- A handlebar bag, a pannier, or a fanny pack is convenient for carrying money, rain gear, snacks, a camera, sunscreen, and insect repellent (useful when the greenhead flies are biting in July and August). Many bags come with a transparent vinyl cover for easy reading of directions and maps.
- Although none of these rides takes you too far away from bicycle shops and gas stations, we recommend you carry a pump, spare inner tube, patch kit, and basic tools such as an Allen wrench set, tire levels, an adjustable wrench, and a Phillips and a regular screwdriver.
- Some people, especially families with children, find a first-aid kit a necessity or, at least, a comfort. Band-Aids, gauze bandages, aspirin, antiseptic, and individually packaged moist towelettes can be kept in a kit and replenished as needed.
- There is relief for cyclists who get saddle-sore (and there are many): Use a gel bicycle saddle or wear padded cycling shorts.
- Always carry a water bottle and light snacks with you, even though you'll rarely be far from stores or public buildings with water fountains. To avoid heat exhaustion, drink regularly, whether you're thirsty or not. Eat small amounts of food throughout the day to maintain a high energy level. Your body will be working hard enough without digesting large amounts of food (exceptions can be made for the best fried clams you've ever tasted).

Bicycling Safety

- Move at your own pace to enjoy your ride. When coasting downhill, keep your weight to the back of the saddle and gently pump your brakes to slow down. Watch for sand or loose gravel on these tours, especially at corners.
- Look ahead for obstacles. Scan the road or path for cracks, debris, potholes, glass, and sand. Watch out for road drains and abrupt drops between the road and shoulder. Check for traffic behind you, using your rearview mirror, before steering around any obstacles. Place your wheels perpendicular to railroad crossings and drainage grates, if you have to traverse these hazards.
- Ride single file, as the roads and bike paths are narrow enough. During stops to talk or rest, move well off the traveled surface. Be sure you can be seen by approaching traffic. Allow an ample distance between your bike and the bicycle ahead.
- Let motorists, other bicyclists, and pedestrians know your intent to turn, pass, or stop by using hand signals or spoken warnings. It's common courtesy to say "bike back" and to slow down to pass pedestrians on a bike path, or to alert cyclists near you of approaching cars from the rear or ahead.
- If a dog chases you, stay calm and dismount, placing the bicycle between you and the dog. Pointing at the dog, shout "stay" or "go home" as if you really mean it. After the dog has calmed down and turned away, walk away slowly without turning your back to it. Never attempt to outpedal a dog or to spray a dog with water or repellent from your bicycle. You may fall or aggravate the dog to attack the cyclist after you—or both.
- Be aware that loose clothing, from shoelaces to pant legs, may catch in moving bike parts. Shoelaces should be double-tied and tucked into your shoes to keep them from wrapping around pedals.
- Brakes don't work well on wet roads that may be covered with a slippery layer of grease and oil. Test your brakes frequently and pump them lightly well in advance of your planned stop. In the fall, wet leaves can make roads hazardous. On Cape Cod and the islands, watch out for sand year-round; it's blown by the wind and left by snowplows and sanders.

Resources

The Massachusetts Office of Travel and Tourism can be reached at 100 Cambridge St., 13th Floor, Boston, MA 02202; 1-800-447-MASS; www. mass-vacation.com/index.shtml.

Contact the Cape Cod Chamber of Commerce at Hyannis, MA 02601, 508-362-3225; www.capecodchamber.org. Each Cape town also has its own chamber of commerce or board of trade as well as brochures, maps, and listings of lodgings. The information centers are open daily in summer, and on weekends during the shoulder seasons.

Contact the Martha's Vineyard Chamber of Commerce at P.O. Box 1698, Vineyard Haven, MA 02568; 508-693-0085; www.myv.com.

Contact the Nantucket Chamber of Commerce at Nantucket, MA 02554, 508-228-1700.

Cape Cod, Martha's Vineyard, and Nantucket: An Explorer's Guide, a good guide to this region, is available at bookstores or from The Countryman Press at 1-800-245-4151.

The official *Arrow Cape Cod Street Atlas* includes Martha's Vineyard and Nantucket. It's a good guide with basic information about points of interest in each town. To order contact the Langenscheidt Publishing Group at 508-279-1177.

Welcome to the Island of Martha's Vineyard is a good map that shows the island, with inserts for the various towns, information about island shuttles and buses and off-island ferries. It's available free from the Martha's Vineyard Commission, 508-693-3453.

North Shore & Cape Cod Bicycle Map, a regional map showing popular bike routes in this area, with information about bicycle repair shops, places to stay, and beaches to see, is available in most local bike or bookshops.

Ferry Lines

Woods Hole, Martha's Vineyard, and Nantucket Steamship Authority, between Hyannis and Nantucket and between Woods Hole and either Oak Bluffs or Vineyard Haven on Martha's Vineyard. For information and advance auto reservations, call 508-477-8600, or check www.islandferry.com.

Hy-Line Cruises, serving Martha's Vineyard (Oak Bluffs) and Nantucket from Ocean Street Dock in Hyannis; 508-778-2600; www.hy-linecruies.com.

Island Queen, Martha's Vineyard (Oak Bluffs) from Falmouth, 75 Falmouth Heights Road, Falmouth; 508-548-4800; www.islandqueen.com.

Falmouth Ferry, serving Falmouth and Martha's Vineyard (Edgartown), 278 Scranton Ave., Falmouth; 508-548-9400.

Schamonchi Ferry, serving New Bedford and Martha's Vineyard (Vineyard Haven), E. Rodney French Blvd., New Bedford; 508-997-1688.

Freedom Cruise Line, express ferry between Nantucket and Harwichport, Route 28, Saquatucket Harbor, Harwichport; 508-432-8999; www.capecod.net/freedom.

Bay State Cruise Co., serving Provincetown and Boston, 164 Northern Ave., World Trade Center, Commonwealth Pier, Boston; 617-748-1428.

Further Reading

Sandwich: A Cape Cod Town, R. A. Lovell (Town of Sandwich, 1984).

The Book of Falmouth, ed. Mary Lou Smith (Falmouth Historical Com., 1986).

Epitaph and Icon, D. H. George and M. A. Nelson (Parnassus Imprints, 1983).

Cranberry Harvest, ed. J. D. Thomas (Spinnaker Publications, 1990).

Indians on Old Cape Cod, Marion Vuilleumier (W. S. Sullwold, 1970).

Names of the Land, E. Green and W. Sachse (Globe Pequot Press, 1983).

A History of Early Orleans, Ruth L. Barnard (Orleans Historical Society, 1975).

Brewster: A Cape Cod Town Remembered (Brewster Historical Society, 1976).

History of Barnstable County, ed. Simon Deyo (H. W. Blake Co., 1890).

Cape Cod National Park Handbook, Robert Finch (U.S. Gov. Printing Office, 1995).

The Outermost House, Henry Beston (Owl Books, repr. 1992).

Monomoy Wilderness (Massachusetts Audubon Society).

The Wampanoag Indian Federation, M. A. Travers (Christopher Publishing, 1957).

Mashpee, The Story of Cape Cod's Indian Town, F. G. Hutchins (Amarta Press, 1979).

Three Centuries of Centerville Scenes, C. F. Herberger (Centerville Historical Society, 1989).

Seven Villages of Barnstable (Town of Barnstable, 1976).

Wellfleet, A Pictorial History, Judy Stetson (Wellfleet Historical Society, 1963).

A Geologist's View of Cape Cod, Arthur N. Strahler (Natural History Press, 1966).

Cape Cod, A Pictorial History, Marion Vuilleumier (Donning Co., 1982).

THE UPPER CAPE

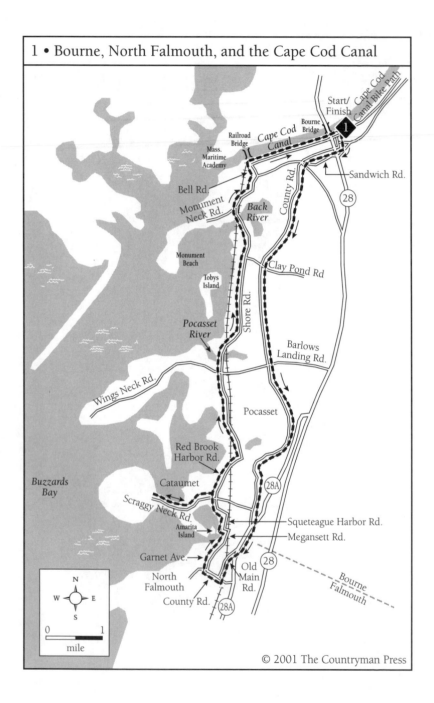

1 • Bourne, North Falmouth, and the Cape Cod Canal

Start/ Finish

Cape Cod Canal Bike Path

Bourne Bridge

Railroad Bridge

Cape Cod Canal

Mass. Maritime Academy

Sandwich Rd.

(28)

Bell Rd.

Monument Neck Rd.

Back River

County Rd.

Monument Beach

Clay Pond Rd

Tobys Island

Shore Rd.

Pocasset River

Barlows Landing Rd.

Wings Neck Rd.

Pocasset

Red Brook Harbor Rd.

Cataumet

Buzzards Bay

(28A)

Scraggy Neck Rd.

Amarita Island

Squeteague Harbor Rd.

Megansett Rd.

Garnet Ave.

Old Main Rd.

(28)

North Falmouth

Bourne Falmouth

County Rd.

(28A)

N
W E
S

0   1
mile

© 2001 The Countryman Press

1
Bourne, North Falmouth, and the Cape Cod Canal

Distance: *18.2 miles*
Terrain: *Flat to gently rolling*

The youngest of the Cape's 15 towns, Bourne is the entry to all of Cape Cod and a good introduction to its history.

Bourne's fate is to be a town of many parts. Bourne was part of Sandwich until 1884. By 1914, the digging of the Cape Cod Canal to join the Manomet and Scusset Rivers split the town into parts now linked by three bridges. In 1935, a major part of Bourne was set aside for the 9,000-acre Massachusetts Military Reservation, including the Veterans' Cemetery.

This tour takes you on a loop through Bourne's coastal villages on the Cape Cod side of the canal. Names like Pocasset and Cataumet and even Monument (from Manomet) reflect the Native American culture that early settlers adopted. The town itself was named in honor of Jonathan Bourne, an influential legislator and native son. By the time of Bourne's death in 1894, his namesake town was known for shipbuilding, international trade, and as a growing summer resort and harbor.

Park at the Bourne Recreation Area parking lot at the base of the Bourne Bridge off Sandwich Road. Public restrooms are available here.

Before starting the tour, walk down to the canal bike path. You'll be standing almost directly under one of the huge supports of the Bourne Bridge, which was built in 1933. The canal itself was opened in 1914, eliminating for ships the hazardous 165-mile trip around Cape Cod. Bought by the federal government of the United States in 1928, the 17-mile-long canal was expanded in 1940.

You'll most likely witness boats coping with the sea-level canal's 6-mph tidal currents, anglers fishing along its riprap banks, walkers and bikers and in-line skaters enjoying the canal path, the salt air, and seabirds. You might be lucky enough to see a seal. The scenic railroad bridge hovering over the canal can be glimpsed in the distance.

0.0 *Heading out of the recreation area, turn right onto Sandwich Road.*

Traffic can be heavy, so you might want to use the sidewalk.

0.3 *The Bourne Post Office and Bourne United Methodist Church are on your right.*

0.5 *The Jonathan Bourne Public Library is on your right. Just beyond is a five-way intersection with a blinking stoplight and a shopping plaza on the left. Go straight through the intersection onto County Road.*

Stop to admire the Briggs-McDermott House, the yellow Greek Revival building on the left.

County Road curves gently back and forth, winding through the countryside with houses on both sides.

1.4 *Pedal by Edward Bradley Park on the right.*

2.2 *Clay Pond Road is to your left, Beach Street to your right.*

2.5 *An old cemetery is on your right. The oldest headstone dates from 1750.*

2.8 *Another old cemetery is on your right.*

This section of the tour has stone walls, gently rolling terrain, and pine trees. Pass a pond, sometimes with swans.

3.1 *Here you come to a stoplight at Barlows Landing Road. You're now in the village of Pocasset.*

4.2 *You'll see a third old cemetery, on your left. There can be heavy traffic at times, so use caution.*

4.6 *The Pocasset Golf Club is on your right, next to a community health center.*

4.9 *You'll pass the former county hospital, originally a tuberculosis hospital, as you ride toward Red Brook Harbor and Buzzards Bay beyond.*

The bay, named for ospreys rather than vultures, was a rendezvous for convoys to the North Atlantic during World War II.

5.4 A small road intersects on your left.

Also on your left, you can see a small cranberry bog, and beyond that a farm. Then a pretty view opens onto several larger cranberry bogs, run by the Handy family, cranberry growers on the Cape for generations.

5.8 There's a cemetery to your right, across from the Cataumet Methodist Church.

The church has been moved twice since its construction in 1765 on what's now the opposite side of the canal.

6.1 Shore Road intersects from your right as you enter the village of Cataumet, meaning "a great fishing place."

There's a lovely old barn on your right with matching gables, large double front doors, and a cupola. The barn was built in the days when large farms were common in this area.

6.6 Here the road curves sharply to your right.

7.1 Merge with Route 28A coming in from your left.

There's a coffee shop and an ice cream shop on your right, open summers only. The Courtyard Restaurant & Pub is on your left. You are now on 28A heading south. This is a busy road; use caution. There's a sidewalk on your right if you'd rather not ride on the road.

7.3 Enter the town of Falmouth.

7.5 Turn right onto Old Main Road toward North Falmouth and Megansett Harbor. Go underneath the old railroad bridge with its 12-foot clearance and stone buttresses.

This is a narrow country road with overhanging trees and old Cape Cod houses.

8.0 Here you come to a blinking yellow light at County Road. On your left is the North Falmouth Superette. On your right is Art's Bike Shop. Turn right onto County Road.

You'll pass the Megansett Harbor Company store, which sells an eclectic assortment of hardware, marine and farm items, and gifts.

8.1 Pass a town playground and ball field. Just ahead, make sure to turn right onto Garnet Avenue, a narrow residential road with large old homes.

8.6 *Here you see a tidal marsh on your left and, a bit farther, a view of the water where you can see boats lying at anchor.*

The road becomes Megansett Road as you reenter Bourne. The neck of land to your left is Amarita Island, the estate of box-toe-shoe inventor and animal lover Thomas Baxendale. When he died in 1910, he left his island, with its monuments to his beloved pets, to the Animal Rescue League of Boston, which sold the land to private owners in 1951.

9.1 *Turn left onto Squeteague Harbor Road.*

Here you should see great water views toward Buzzards Bay, where the squeteague, or weakfish, was common.

9.3 *Turn left, staying on Squeteague Harbor Road; Mystery Lane goes off to your right at this point.*

9.4 *Turn left onto Scraggy Neck Road through the area formerly known as Scraggs Neck, named after the scraggly thickets that covered the land.*

10.2 *Stop at a gate that opens only for private residents and their guests.*

Here you'll be treated to great views of the boat harbor and Buzzards Bay. Unless it's foggy, you should be able to see one of the big channel markers out in the bay. Return along Scraggy Neck Road.

10.9 *Turn left onto Red Brook Harbor Road. This is the intersection where you turned from Squeteague Harbor Road onto Scraggy Neck Road.*

You're now on a winding road with excellent water views.

11.5 *Pass through Parker's Boat Yard with boats of every description on both sides of the road.*

In the mid-1800s, packet boats would dock here to ferry passengers and freight between the Cape and New Bedford, Marion, and Mattapoisett across the bay.

11.8 *Turn left onto Shore Road.*

Immediately on your right is Red Brook Pond. The Bourne Conservation Trust owns 40 acres here, home to Massachusetts's state flower, the trailing arbutus, and many walking trails. Cross the

Herring River, named after the herrings and alewives that swim upstream to spawn in the pond each spring.

The road curves to your right, goes uphill, and then winds gently through this scenic coastal area.

12.1 *Pass under the railroad tracks. Take the sidewalk on your left if you feel the road is too busy.*

13.1 *Cross Barlows Landing Road.*

At this four-way stop there's a pizza place on your left and a restaurant-bakery and convenience store on your right.

You can take a short detour down Wings Neck by turning left onto Barlows Landing Road, which becomes Wings Neck Road. Named after an early Sandwich settler, Wings Neck was popular in the 1880s among wealthy families who built palatial summer cottages here.

13.3 *Cross a small bridge straddling the Pocasset River, and then curve around with the river to your right.*

Once known as Barlow's River, named after one of many iron factories along its banks, this tidal river is now specially protected as a state area of critical environmental concern. On your left are lovely views of salt marshes and Buzzards Bay beyond.

14.0 *Here you'll be treated to nice views of the water and Wings Neck to your left.*

14.5 *Briarwood Conference Center and Retreat is on your left.*

15.0 *Pass Tobys Island on your left. Its shape creates a protected boat harbor.*

15.2 *On your left you can see the old train depot. Curve around to your right past a Cumberland Farms convenience store, then immediately turn left and pass Perry's Boat Yard on your right.*

15.9 *With Cape Marine on your left, cross over the Back River on a small bridge.*

You pass the Fish Market and Lobster Trap Company on your left and lovely water and marsh views to your right. You also pass a cemetery with several gravestones from the 1830s.

16.4 *Pass Monument Neck Road on your left.*

This part of town is known as Gray Gables, the name of President Grover Cleveland's estate from 1890 to 1904.

(Turn left and follow Presidents Road to Mashnee Neck for a view of the canal and beaches.)

16.6 *Turn left onto Bell Road. This takes you to the Tidal Flats Recreation Area by the Cape Cod Canal.*

16.8 *At the junction, turn right to travel through the parking lot and find the bike path.*

To the left there's a small parking lot, bathrooms, picnic tables and a great view. Across the canal, to the left, is the Massachusetts Maritime Academy. Straight ahead is a small boat basin where you'll often see tugboats.

Turning to the right, toward the silver railroad bridge, cross the tracks and walk your bike up to the Cape Cod Canal Bike Path.

16.9 *Pass by the 544-foot-wide railroad bridge with its silver towers.*

This bridge was built in 1933, along with the Sagamore and Bourne Bridges. The entire track and bed, counterbalanced with enormous weights in the two towers on land, lowers into place when needed for rail traffic.

17.3 *On your left you can glimpse the Aptucxet Museum, now operated by the Bourne Historical Society.*

The Aptucxet trading post was established in 1627 to encourage trade among Plymouth settlers, Native Americans, and Dutch merchants in New York. The Pilgrims needed to repay debt to the London merchants who financed their trip to the New World. The historical society built this replica in the 1920s.

18.2 *Return to the Bourne Bridge. On your right is the parking lot where the tour started.*

Bicycle Repair Services

Art's Bike Shop, 70 County Road, North Falmouth, MA 508-563-7379

Corner Cycle, 115 Palmer Ave. (Route 28), Falmouth, MA 508-540-4195

True Wheel Cycle, Route 28, Pocasset, MA 508-564-4807

2
Falmouth and Woods Hole

Distance: *26.4 miles*
Terrain: *Flat to gently rolling*

Lined by miles of beaches and laced with shady roads that dip past small harbors, Falmouth has satisfied visitors since Bartholomew Gosnold dropped anchor here in 1602.

In 1686, the town was named after Gosnold's home port in England. This area's Native American heritage remains in names such as Acapesket and Quisset. Each of Falmouth's nine villages has its own flavor, its own history, its own fiercely partisan supporters.

Thousands of visitors pass through Falmouth yearly to catch Woods Hole ferries to Martha's Vineyard, Nantucket, and the Elizabeth Islands. Scientists compete to study and research here, on the cutting edge of marine science. Professional and weekend athletes love to run the Falmouth Road Race—it's fun and short enough to be an adventure instead of a test of endurance.

Along Vineyard Sound you can see the former summer cottages, now year-round homes, that are left from the days when trains brought summer visitors to shore resorts. You go by stately mansions and along the scenic harbors of Buzzards Bay, once filled with working schooners and now dotted with private yachts. You can visit long sandy beaches beloved by college kids and families finding their place in the sun.

This tour begins at the North Falmouth Public Library. To get there from the Cape side of the Bourne Bridge, take Route 28 south toward Falmouth and Woods Hole. Take the Route 151/North Falmouth exit. At the bottom of the exit ramp, turn left onto Route 151 toward the village of North Falmouth.

Go straight at the traffic light and straight at the next stop sign. You'll now be on County Road. Go past the baseball field on your left, then bear left on Chester Street. The North Falmouth Library is on your left.

0.0 Leaving the North Falmouth Library parking lot, turn left onto Chester Street.

This is a narrow, winding, shady road with light traffic. Enjoy a glimpse of Cedar Lake on your left.

0.8 At the stop sign go straight across Wild Harbor Road and onto Quaker Road, a marked bike route.

1.6 Curley Boulevard comes in on your left.

Pass St. Elizabeth Seton Church on your left and, on your right, the Sea Crest Resort.

2.5 As you round a corner, Old Silver Beach fills the horizon.

Named in 1897 after its silvery sand, this ever-popular area is one of the first public beaches after you cross the bridges. There's a bathhouse, swimming, and an excellent vegetarian snack bar.

Traffic clogs this road in the summer as beachgoers wait in line. There are sidewalks available as you pedal uphill.

3.7 Veer left onto Nashawena Street and cross a bridge over West Falmouth Harbor.

3.9 Check out the view of West Falmouth Harbor, its boats in the marina, and the Victorian summer cottages on shore.

The mansions date from the stable, prosperous era between the Civil War and World War I.

4.3 At the stop sign, turn right onto Old Dock Road, a narrow and busy road that leads to a town landing and marina.

4.7 At the stop sign, turn left onto Chapoquoit Road.

As you turn, note the Queen Ann–style home of the College Light Opera Company, a popular summer troupe. For a scenic side trip, turn right to Chapoquoit Beach, just 0.4 mile away, and a view across the blue harbor, white with sails. The narrow strip of beach below the seawall is a great place for walking.

5.0 Turn right onto Route 28A, a busy road previously known simply as the Shore Road.

5.5 Here you come to the Chapoquoit Grille, an excellent restaurant.

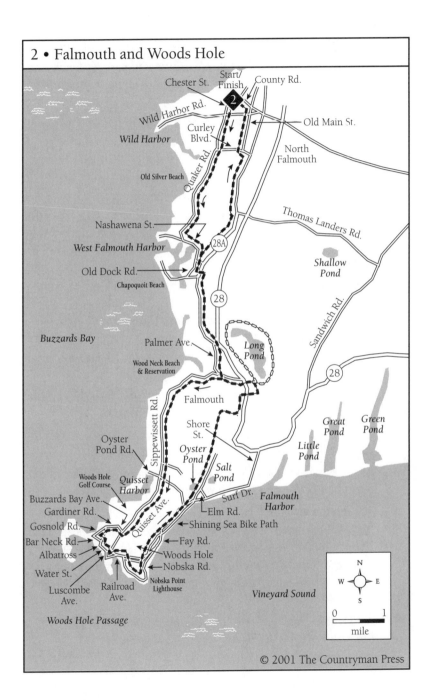

2 • Falmouth and Woods Hole

Chester St.
Start/Finish
County Rd.
2
Wild Harbor Rd.
Old Main St.
Curley Blvd.
Wild Harbor
North Falmouth
Quaker Rd.
Old Silver Beach
Thomas Landers Rd.
Nashawena St.
28A
West Falmouth Harbor
Shallow Pond
Old Dock Rd.
Sandwich Rd.
Chapoquoit Beach
28
Buzzards Bay
Palmer Ave.
Long Pond
Wood Neck Beach & Reservation
28
Falmouth
Shore St.
Great Pond
Green Pond
Oyster Pond Rd.
Oyster Pond
Sippewissett Rd.
Salt Pond
Little Pond
Woods Hole Golf Course
Quisset Harbor
Surf Dr.
Falmouth Harbor
Buzzards Bay Ave.
Quisset Ave.
Gardiner Rd.
Elm Rd.
Gosnold Rd.
Shining Sea Bike Path
Bar Neck Rd.
Fay Rd.
Albatross
Woods Hole
Water St.
Nobska Rd.
Luscombe Ave.
Railroad Ave.
Nobska Point Lighthouse
Vineyard Sound
Woods Hole Passage

N
W—E
S

0   1
mile

© 2001 The Countryman Press

6.2 *Turn right onto Palmer Avenue at the flashing yellow light.*

6.4 *On your left is Peach Tree Circle, where you can get lunch and fresh produce in season. Stay on Palmer Avenue as it winds to the bottom of a hill.*

7.2 *Turn right onto Sippewissett Road and climb uphill.*

You are now on the Claire Saltsonstall Bikeway from Boston to Cape Cod, which curves around Little Sippewissett Lake.

7.7 *You'll pass Wood Neck Road on your right.*

This inviting road leads through wild grapes and rose mallows to a beach. If you stay on Sippewissett, you'll enjoy the beautiful view. Its classic half-Capes and three-quarter Capes will test your fractions. A full Cape has a central door with two windows on each side. A half-Cape has a door and two windows on one side. A three-quarter Cape? Two windows on one side of the door; a single window on the other side.

10.1 *Here you'll come to a stop sign. Cross Oyster Pond Road, leaving the Saltsonstall bike route.*

The road now becomes Quisset Avenue, named after a tribe of Native Americans from this area. There are a number of estates here, established in the early 1900s, and a yacht club. If you turned right at the stop sign mentioned above, you'd travel out to a point of land known as the Knob. The outer part of this point is a nature preserve.

This shady, sheltered road leads to the scientific and maritime center of Woods Hole. You'll pass the National Academy of Sciences in Woods Hole. Over a hedge you can just glimpse Quisset Harbor.

11.1 *After biking up Golf Course Hill, you see the entrance to Woods Hole Golf Course, a private club established in 1899.*

11.5 *Near the bottom of the hill, turn right onto Buzzards Bay Avenue, which winds through a long-established village neighborhood.*

11.7 *At the stop sign turn left onto Gardiner Road. Here you can see views of Quisset Harbor over a low seawall.*

12.0 Bear right onto Gosnold Road and curve around a small point of land.

12.3 With the mansions of Penzance Point before you, turn left onto Bar Neck Road.

When it was an island, in the mid-1800s, this peninsula was rich with smells of the guano and menhadens mixed here and sold as fertilizer by the Pacific Guano Company. Now the point is richly settled with private estates. The old shipyards of Bar Neck launched many whalers and trading ships.

12.4 At the stop sign, turn right onto Albatross Street and go past the National Oceanic and Atmospheric Administration's aquarium, with its outdoor seal tank (feedings are at 11 AM and 4 PM).

12.5 Turn left onto Water Street.

Pass by the Marine Biological Laboratory and the Woods Hole Oceanographic Institution, two internationally known research centers.

The oldest institution here is the National Marine Fisheries Laboratory, making Woods Hole a scientists' mecca since 1871. In the 1990s, Bob Ballard launched his expedition to the sunken *Titanic* from Woods Hole, and from here the submersible *Alvin* leaves to make its deep dives to map the vents off the Galapagos Islands. The influx of researchers from around the world creates a fascinating mix of cultures in Woods Hole, which is also the gateway to Martha's Vineyard and Nantucket by ferry. Small surprise that the village supports a thriving folk coffeehouse and an experimental theater.

Travel over the drawbridge past the Fishmonger's Restaurant, a good place to soak up fluids and village atmosphere. The bridge was built across Eel Pond to connect the businesses on Water Street to the homes of Woods Hole.

12.8 Turn right onto Luscombe Avenue.

Pass by the many shops, or stop at Jimmy's Restaurant for a tasty lobster roll.

Straight ahead is the terminal of the Woods Hole Steamship Authority, which offers ferries to Martha's Vineyard and Nantucket.

Susan Milton

Little Harbor in Woods Hole, one of the Cape's scenic harbors

There are rest rooms inside the terminal and a bus shelter outside for rides to Hyannis, Boston, and New York. The ferry docks to your right. Ferry service here began as an extension of rail service in 1873.

As you turn left on Railroad Avenue, notice the chain-link fence that marks the entrance to the Shining Sea Bike Path, a scenic ride from Woods Hole to the historic center of Falmouth. You'll join the trail later, after a trip to see the stunning Nobska Lighthouse.

12.9 Ride up the hill, past the trail entrance, on Railroad Avenue. Turn right at the top of the hill back onto Water Street, which becomes Woods Hole Road.

There's a sidewalk on your right overlooking Little Harbor and the Coast Guard docks. On a nearby estate, gardener Michael Walsh developed the rambler rose.

13.1 Turn right onto Church Street. As you cross a bridge, look down to the bike trail in the ferry parking lot below.

The stone Church of the Messiah was the original church for the first Episcopalian parish here.

13.4 Here you coast downhill into a picture-postcard view of the

lighthouse, the keeper's cottage, and passing ferries to the Islands. Climb the hill, where the road narrows, and start down toward the lapping waves of Vineyard Sound. The road soon becomes Nobska Road.

In 1797, the isolated point was home to a smallpox hospital. The lighthouse was built in 1829.

14.4 *You will approach a bridge over Nobska Road. Slow down and, after the bridge, look to your left for the path back up to the Shining Sea Bike Path. Walk up the path and turn toward Falmouth, heading away from Woods Hole and the ferry parking lot.*

This path, built on an old railbed, is popular with commuters on skates, bicycles, and feet. On the pavement, notice cryptic notations about geologic time. It's a display, using distance, to show the span of the earth's development.

15.3 *Emerge out of woods to sniff the salty air of Vineyard Sound. Hear the rocks at the water's edge clatter under the waves. Take a rest and listen.*

15.8 *Pass a memorial to celebrate the 100th anniversary of the song "America the Beautiful," written by Falmouth native Katharine Lee Bates.*

A replica of the memorial is on top of Pikes Peak, Colorado, where in July 1893 Bates was inspired by what she saw. She wrote the words soon afterward in her hotel in Colorado Springs.

15.9 *Veer to your right past Oyster Pond, which was an inlet until the road cut off its sea access.*

The tree-lined trail leads past climbing bittersweet, roses, and chokecherries. Check out the flower and vegetable garden to your left just before Elm Road.

16.5 *Cross Elm Road.*

To see more of the shore, turn right and, at the stop sign, turn left onto Surf Drive.

Pass Salt Pond on your left and, to your right, houses on stilts that lift them above hurricane tides that engulf this beach. The large painted numbers in the road are mile markers from the road race. Return to the bike path.

17.0 *Enjoy the pond, often home to swans, from the benches on the right.*

17.8 *Dismount and cross Locust Road, which later becomes Woods Hole Road.*

There are picnic tables, water, and toilets here, once the end of the bike trail. The 300 Committee in the nearby office building has led local efforts to buy and preserve land in Falmouth. Stop by its office for the latest map of land and trails.

18.2 *Curve to the left to cross the railroad tracks at the depot.*

18.5 *As the trail ends, turn right into the ferry parking lot, pass the ice rink and stop at Route 28, here known as Palmer Avenue.*

The parking lot is one of several satellite lots for the ferries at Woods Hole. To your left are restaurants and the chamber of commerce, a good place for information.

18.6 *Turn left and stay on the sidewalk. At the stoplight, cross Jones Road.*

19.1 *Look for two stone pillars on the right. Cross the road and pass through them to enter Goodwill Park.*

In 1894, Joseph Story Fay, a wealthy summer visitor, gave the public 70 acres of land for horseback riding and walking. The town-owned park is an oasis in Falmouth and a starting point for exploring north along the Buzzards Bay moraine.

19.2 *Turn left immediately and follow the paved road through the park.*

Or ride straight for 0.2 mile to the parking area and gate to the trail along Long Pond. This 150-acre pond supplies a majority of Falmouth's drinking water supply. The circular trail covers 3.5 miles on a mix of dirt roads and footpaths. You will see bogs, the rare Plymouth gentian, and possibly a bald eagle or two. The trail is just part of a 10-mile-long trail along the rocky moraine to Route 151 and the wildlife reservation there.

19.4 *At the water department, turn left. At Route 28/Palmer Avenue, dismount and cross carefully. Stay on the sidewalk and turn left as Palmer Avenue veers away to the west. Cross over the railroad tracks.*

20.1 *Veer right, away from Sippiwisset Road, to stay on Palmer Avenue.*

21.1 *Turn left on Route 28A.*

21.8 *Cross Brick Kiln Road.*

22.5 *Pass through West Falmouth, one of the town's nine original villages.*

You'll see the library as well as many shops and galleries.

24.0 *Pass by historic Bourne Farm at the junction with Thomas Landers Road.*

The land for this farm was cleared more than 200 years ago. The house is one of the seven oldest in Falmouth. The 40-acre farm, now on the National Register of Historic Places, was bought in 1980 by Salt Pond Area Bird Sanctuaries, Inc.

25.0 *As you travel around the rotary, follow signs to Old Silver Beach and Shore Road. Exit onto Curley Boulevard.*

25.3 *Turn right onto Old Main Street. Pass a school on your left.*

Cross the intersection of Wild Harbor Road on your left and pass through Nye Village, where there were once 24 Nye homes within this mile-long stretch of road.

26.4 *Turn left onto County Road at the blinking yellow light near the North Falmouth Superette. Bear left onto Chester Street at the five-way intersection.*

You'll soon come to the North Falmouth parking lot on your left and the tour's end.

Bicycle Repair Services

Art's Bike Shop, 70 County Road, North Falmouth, MA 508-563-7379

Corner Cycle, 115 Palmer Ave. (Route 28), Falmouth, MA 508-540-4195

True Wheel Cycle, Route 28, Pocasset, MA 508-564-4807

3

Sandwich and the Cape Cod Canal

Distance: 18.6 miles
Terrain: Mostly flat, with a few hills

This tour starts in Bourne, which was part of Sandwich until 1884, and offers an easy ride along the world's widest canal—or you can race the freighters, tug-pushed barges, and fishing boats that travel between Cape Cod Bay and Buzzards Bay.

In the historic village of Sandwich, you'll ride into the past beloved by naturalist-writer Thornton Burgess, who grew up here and returned in his later years. You can learn more about his life and about the settings for his Peter Rabbit stories at the Thornton Burgess Museum and the Green Briar Nature Center.

The Sandwich Glass Museum traces the development of the glass industry that started here in 1824 and grew to employ 500 people working four shifts around the clock. The museum itself draws thousands of visitors each year to admire its fine collections of pressed, molded, and blown glass. This thriving industry brought the railroad to Sandwich and employed Irish workers who started the first Catholic church on the Cape. Now you can watch present-day glassblowers at work at the Pairpoint Crystal Company along the canal as they make modern glassware, also valued as collectibles.

At Heritage Plantation, near the village center, the main draw is the Dexter rhododendrons in the spring, as well as antique cars, a windmill, and other Americana.

This scenic tour starts at the Bourne Recreation Area (see Tour 1), directly beneath the Bourne Bridge. Rest rooms are available here.

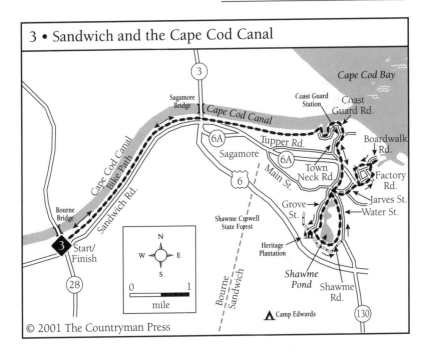

3 • Sandwich and the Cape Cod Canal

© 2001 The Countryman Press

0.0 *Heading out of the recreation area, turn right onto the Cape Cod Canal Bike Path, heading toward Sandwich.*

Before you turn, look to your left and you'll see the historic railroad bridge.

0.9 *Note the blue water tower to your left across the canal.*

There are benches all along the canal, or you can sit anywhere on its grassy banks. At 8 mph, you'll ride neck and neck with Coast Guard boats and fishing boats in the canal's currents. Gulls and cormorants perch on utility poles all along the canal.

2.2 *Across the canal you can see the Bournedale herring run, a source of food, bait, and fertilizer for Native Americans, colonists, and present-day residents.*

Each April and May herrings and alewives still leap up the run to return to their spawning grounds after two or three years at sea.

2.3 *The U.S. Army Corps of Engineers Herring Run Visitors Center is directly across the canal.*

The center is open year-round from 9 AM to dusk and offers exhibits about the canal and interpretive programs.

3.3 Pass underneath the Sagamore Bridge between the concrete buttresses.

To your right you'll see the railroad track headed for the Canal Electric power plant, supplier of electricity to New England since 1968. A second unit was added in 1974 and recently converted from coal to natural gas. The plant's 500-foot towers are a landmark for mariners and beachgoers as far away as Provincetown.

A short distance inland, on Sandwich Road, you'll find the Pairpoint Crystal Company, where you can watch artisans blow glass and buy a memento of your visit.

3.7 You can see railroad tracks to your right, next to the service road and bike path.

Watch for the vintage dining cars and passenger coaches of the Cape Cod Scenic Railroad, which makes trips from Hyannis to the canal May through October.

4.7 Pass a round fuel-storage tank used for the electric plant. The service road runs next to the bike path here.

5.1 Turn right at the power plant for a good view past the canal out to Cape Cod Bay.

This is a popular fishing spot. From here you can spot the navigational markers at the entrance to the canal.

5.3 The bike path ends at the Sandwich Recreation Area. Leave this area on the main entrance road.

5.4 Turn left onto Ed Moffit Drive at the end of the boat basin. Go around the parking lot, which provides storage for pleasure boats in the off-season. Pass the Bulkhead Recreation Area's parking lot on the other side of the boat basin.

5.8 On your right is the U.S. Coast Guard Station. Turn right onto Coast Guard Road.

With the widening of the Cape Cod Canal in 1935, this station moved inland to preside over the new boat basin. Enlarged in 1963, the basin harbors an active fishing fleet.

6.0 Turn right onto Town Neck Road.

Use the sidewalk on your right if traffic is heavy.

6.3 Using caution, cross the railroad tracks and turn left onto Tupper Road.

Use the sidewalk on your left if traffic is heavy. You can see the tall stack of the power plant to your right.

6.6 Continue across Route 6A on Tupper Road.

Be careful here—Route 6A is heavily traveled. Pass the Compass Bank. You're now entering Historic Sandwich Village, established in 1639 and named after its resemblance to Sandwich, England, an embarkation point to America.

A pretty marsh lies to your left, 17th-century homes and inns to your right. Ahead you can see the tall spire of the First Church of Christ, inspired by a Christopher Wren design.

6.9 Cross Main Street, with the town hall on your left, to Grove Street.

If you have the time, stop for a little time-traveling before you cross Main Street. On your left is the Sandwich Glass Museum and its displays of 150 examples of the glass made between 1825 and 1888. The museum is open 9:30–4:30 daily April through October, and Wednesday through Sunday in winter. It's closed in January. Call 508-888-0251 for more information.

The town hall, built in 1834, is still the center of government. Look for the water bubbler to your left, set in a stone landing. People from on- and off-Cape fill their water jugs from this artesian well.

Beyond the town hall is lovely Shawme Pond, complete with ducks and often a rowboat or canoe.

7.1 The Old Town Cemetery lies on your left, with oak trees overhanging the pond.

The oldest gravestone dates back to 1683 in this cemetery, which offers some of the best epitaphs and icons on the Cape.

7.7 Another old cemetery is on your right.

Here you can glimpse the big round dairy barn at Heritage Plantation to your left. Go and see the 1930 Duesenberg, once owned

Kevin & Nan Jeffrey

The Sandwich Glass Museum

by movie star Gary Cooper, or the 1912 carousel. The museum and gardens, and a very good snack bar and restaurant, are open 10–5, mid-May until late October (508-888-3300).

7.8 *Veer left on the dirt road that skirts the picnic area.*

This road is a bit bumpy but is good for biking, with rolling hills, deep woods, and gentle curves.

8.1 *The dirt road ends here. Continue straight across on Shawme Road (don't take the sharp left downhill on Shaker House Way).*

You'll soon see a sign that says SCENIC ROAD, and you'll probably agree. It's a steady climb until you come to Hilltop Condominiums. Be cautious—this road is pretty but it's also narrow, with many curves.

8.6 *Shaker House Way intersects on your left. Stay on Shawme Road.*

8.8 *Turn left onto Water Street (Route 130).*

This is a busy road, so be careful. You may want to use the sidewalk on your left. The Henry Wing Elementary School is across the street.

9.4 *Riding into Sandwich Center, see the Hoxie House, the oldest house in Sandwich, on your left by Shawme Pond.*

This distinctive saltbox was built about 1637 and bought by the town of Sandwich for restoration in 1960.

9.5 *On your left is the Thornton W. Burgess Museum.*

Thornton W. Burgess left his hometown of Sandwich after high school and returned after a successful career in journalism and writing children's books. Here he found inspiration for his many books and stories about Peter Rabbit and Old Mother West Wind. Before he died in 1965, he had laid the foundation for education about nature and the preservation of open space, including Smiling Pond in his beloved Sandwich.

9.6 *The historic Dexter Grist Mill is on your left.*

A sign by the mill informs visitors, "To this grist mill, the early settlers of Sandwich brought their corn to be ground into meal, their most important food—you will see the old machinery with wooden gears in full operation, grinding corn—fresh ground meal is available." Dexter Grist Mill was established in 1654 and restored in 1961.

9.7 *Turn right at the fork in the road onto Main Street, another historic stretch of road.*

On your left, pass by the Yesteryears Doll Museum, a former church with stained-glass windows of Sandwich glass, and the Dan'l Webster Inn, with its four-star restaurant and fine bar. On your right are a public library, art galleries, and antiques shops.

9.9 *Turn left onto Jarves Street, between the traffic island and the Boston Organ and Piano Company.*

The brick inn on the right was the first Catholic church on Cape Cod, dedicated in 1830. The street is named after the founder of the Boston and Sandwich Glass Company.

10.0 *Cross Route 6A.*

You're riding through the former site of the factory, furnace, tenements, and school of the Boston and Sandwich Glass Company.

10.1 *Cross the railroad tracks and admire the attractive depot on your right.*

10.2 *Turn left onto Factory Road.*

Straight ahead is a plaque that maps the site of the glass company in 1849. The road curves to your right, turning into Boardwalk Road as it travels past cottages and through marshes toward Cape Cod Bay.

10.6 *Enjoy the breathtaking view of the marshes, the dunes along Town Beach, and, of course, the famous boardwalk.*

Built in 1875, the boardwalk was destroyed in a winter storm. It was rebuilt in 1992 by subscribers who paid $40 per plank to restore this local landmark, which bridges the marsh and Mill Creek to Town Beach. It's worth the walk to read the subscribers' names and their messages on the planks, such as WHERE IT ALL BEGAN and RANDOM ACTS.

11.1 *Return on Boardwalk Road, passing by Factory Road. Turn left onto Church Street, then right onto Jarves Street.*

11.3 *Cross Route 6A.*

Russell's Corner Store offers sandwiches and ice cream, if you need some fuel.

11.5 *Veer right onto Main Street.*

11.7 *Turn right onto Tupper Road at the Sandwich Glass Museum.*

18.6 *Retrace your route to the Cape Cod Canal Bike Path and back to the Bourne Recreation Area, where the tour began.*

Bicycle Repair Services

Art's Bike Shop, 70 County Road, North Falmouth, MA 508-563-7379

Cape Cod Bike Rental, Route 6A, Sandwich, MA 508-833-2453

Corner Cycle, 115 Palmer Ave. (Route 28), Falmouth, MA 508-540-4195

True Wheel Cycle, Route 28, Pocasset, MA 508-564-4807

THE MID-CAPE

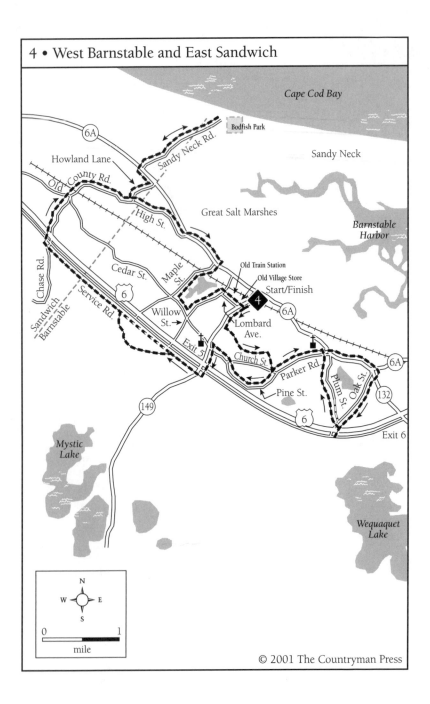

Cape Cod Bay

Bodfish Park

Sandy Neck

6A

Howland Lane

Old County Rd.

Sandy Neck Rd.

High St.

Great Salt Marshes

Barnstable Harbor

Chase Rd.

Cedar St.

Maple St.

Old Train Station

Old Village Store

Start/Finish

4

6A

6

Sandwich
Barnstable

Service Rd.

Willow St.

Lombard Ave.

Exit 5

Church St.

Parker Rd.

6A

Pine St.

Plum St.

Oak St.

132

149

6

Exit 6

Mystic Lake

Wequaquet Lake

N
W → E
S

0   1
mile

© 2001 The Countryman Press

4
West Barnstable and East Sandwich

Distance: *17.8 miles*
Terrain: *Mostly flat, with a few long hills*

Bricks, marshes, and stone walls are a few signs of the history you'll see on this tour of West Barnstable and East Sandwich.

The north side of Barnstable was the first part of town settled by colonists who bought the land from Native Americans in 1639. Like the Wampanoags, led by the sachem Iyanough, the colonists used the nearby Great Salt Marshes along Sandy Neck as a source of fodder, insulation for houses, and mulch. The town's picturesque stone walls are the gift of the glacier that left the stones and boulders for farmers to clear from their fields along the moraine.

Later new settlers came, such as the Finns, emigrants who left the factory towns of Massachusetts in the mid-1800s for Cape jobs on farms, in cranberry bogs, and at the brickyards. They were joined by Cape Verdeans, Irish, and Italians, all of whom left their names on road signs as well as in the telephone book.

West Barnstable bricks are collectibles now, but they were simply a practical necessity in the late 1800s. The factory was near Garretts Pond and Brickyard Creek, with clay pits and sand nearby.

After converting to steam power in 1887, the factory could make 2 million bricks a year. Ever since the factory closed in 1929, its bricks have been salvaged for buildings or walkways, stolen from abandoned properties, and snapped up at yard sales.

This tour begins on Route 149, not far from Route 6A. Park at the Old Village Store, well worth a wander. Nearby is the old train depot and a pizza place.

0.0 *Turn right out of the parking lot onto Route 149 heading south. Pass the Whelden Memorial Library on the right.*

You're leaving the Lombard property, 50 acres of land left to the town's poor in 1735 by 35-year-old Parker Lombard. The poor-house was here, along with the selectmen's office, now a community art gallery, and schoolhouses. On this land you'll also find the library and the community hall and baseball field. The town still earns about $40,000 a year in rents to aid the poor, as Lombard wanted.

0.5 *Turn left into the West Barnstable Fire Station. Ride to the left, behind the building, to find the start of the trail for the 246-acre Bridge Creek Conservation Area.*

The town bought these woods in the 1970s to preserve its mix of habitats for ferns, red maples, tupelos, hollies, and rhododendrons.

Its 2.5 miles of trails pass through a nice mix of terrain—woods, swamps, and fields with bumpy tree roots. This one-mile section of trail may be soggy in certain seasons. Near the end, riders must dismount to travel safely across plank bridges.

Alternate route: For an easier ride, detour 0.2 mile down Route 149. Turn left on Church Street and, in 0.6 mile, rejoin the route at the trail's parking lot.

0.9 *After riding through a tunnel of trees and shrubs, pass a bench and veer left.*

Get ready to bump over the first of many tree roots on this twisty trail.

1.1 *Turn left onto a grassy cartpath.*

Cross the first of six footbridges. Native hollies line the trail.

1.4 *Turn left, away from the stone wall, a boundary wall.*

1.5 *Turn right and climb into the parking lot on Church Street.*

1.6 *Turn left onto Church Street and travel along this densely wooded road with its lovely old stone walls.*

Merge with Parker Road.

2.4 *Turn right onto Route 6A.*

The Church of Our Lady of Hope Chapel, built of West Barnstable bricks, is on your left. You'll also pass enticing crafts shops and the First Lutheran Church.

3.1 *Make a sharp right onto Oak Street.*

This is a busy intersection of Route 6A and Route 132, leading to the Cape Cod Community College.

3.8 *Turn right onto Plum Street, just before the overpass of Route 6.*

This gravelly road bumps back down to Parker Road and passes Garretts Pond on the right. Watch out for cars and go slowly. The curves leave room for only one car.

Andrew Garrett was a Continental Army lieutenant who was a prisoner of war of Native Americans for four years; after the war he lived near this pond, which bears his name. Later this was the site of the brick factory for which West Barnstable was so well known.

You can take a swim at the town landing here. Enjoy the old farm on your left at the bend in the road.

4.7 *Turn left onto Parker Road.*

5.3 *Turn left onto Pine Street.*

Cranberry bogs soon bracket the narrow road, which is shaded by ivy on overhanging trees. You'll travel close to Route 6, the Mid-Cape Highway, here. Rounding a corner, you'll see to the left the pastoral Jenkins Farm, shingled and with white trim, set behind stone walls near a mill pond. The view from the highway is one of the best on the Cape.

6.3 *Turn left onto Church Street after the Crocker Park Cemetery.*

Look ahead and see the West Parish Meetinghouse, the church for which this street is named. The church is nicknamed "The Rooster Church" for the golden weathervane on its top. Built in 1717, it's the oldest Congregational church in the country; its members had first settled in Scituate in 1634, before emigrating to the Cape. Paul Revere cast its 922-pound bell. The church is open to the public.

6.5 *At Route 149, turn left and cross over Route 6.*

6.8 *Turn right onto Service Road.*

Pass by the parking lot on the left for the Trail of Tears through the 1,100-acre West Barnstable Conservation Area.

7.2 Turn left at the next entrance, marked by a yellow gate.

This is just a teaser for the 15 miles of walking and biking trails in this hilly pine and oak forest. Trail maps are available at local libraries and at the conservation commission's office, 367 Main Street, Hyannis.

The only sounds may be from the airfield and the police shooting range, both a comfortable distance away.

Alternate route: For an easier ride, go straight along Service Road to the trail's exit half a mile ahead.

7.9 Emerge from the woods into the cleared power line right-of-way. Veer right onto a trail and make a second right to reenter the woods.

The trails along the power lines are rocky, a reminder that you are traveling through the glacial moraine that created the Cape's spine.

8.1 Turn left off the cartpath onto a narrow trail.

Watch out for overhanging branches on this overgrown section of trail.

8.3 Emerge from the woods, pass the gate, and turn left onto Service Road.

There are some hills on this road as you enter the Ridge District of Sandwich along the glacial moraine. Before that, you'll pass the police shooting range on your left as you bike parallel to the highway. Along this road you reach a high point of Cape Cod, but trees block your view of Cape Cod Bay.

9.7 At the stop sign, turn right onto Chase Road.

Cross the highway and continue on Chase Road (exit 4). The road is paved here but has sharp curves.

10.4 Veer right onto Old County Road. Go over a railroad bridge.

This was part of the original road between Sandwich and Barnstable, laid out in 1685. The woods here are dense, the road narrow and inviting.

10.9 Pass the Hornbeam Farm and its shingled barn with large barn-red doors.

11.2 Turn left onto Howland Lane.

This is a beautiful road with large old houses and stone walls.

Susan Milton

This Federal-style house, built in 1840, is one of the earliest in West Barnstable.

11.5 *Cross the town boundary into Barnstable, just before Route 6A.*

11.6 *Turn left onto Route 6A (use extreme caution here).*

Stop to enjoy the beautiful view of the marshes and Sandy Neck beyond. This barrier beach stretches 7 miles from Scorton Creek, named by Native Americans, through the Great Salt Marshes that protect Barnstable Harbor. Owned by the town, Sandy Neck is maintained as a recreation and conservation resource. Naturalists come here to research turtles, plovers, and deer ticks (the tiny ticks that carry Lyme disease)—and vacationers to try out the latest in bathing gear, fishing lures, and oversand vehicles.

11.8 *To your right is a cluster of gift shops. To your left is the Amari Ristorante.*

11.9 *Turn right onto Sandy Neck Road by a motel named (what else?) the Sandy Neck Motel.*

This road is wide, level, and well traveled in the summer, when people flock to the cool, deep waters off Sandy Neck Beach.

12.6 *Climb a gentle rise and get a lovely view of Cape Cod Bay and Sandy Neck.*

During World War II, the beach was a practice ground for amphibious maneuvers.

12.8 *Pass the ranger station, administered and staffed by the town of Barnstable.*

Note the PLEASE KEEP OFF THE DUNES signs. You can see the Sandwich power plant's 500-foot towers to your left and Plymouth beyond. To your right the shore curves around toward the Cape town of Dennis.

13.1 *The road ends at a parking lot, the entrance to Bodfish Park, which has beach trails for oversand vehicles with permits. Return to Route 6A along the Sandy Neck Road.*

14.3 *Turn left onto Route 6A, return to Howland Lane, and turn right.*

14.9 *Turn left onto Old County Road.*

The road's name changes to High Street here. Soon you cross into Barnstable (signs are confusing at this point). As you rise to a high point on this hilly road, you'll understand how the road got its name.

15.8 *Turn right onto Route 6A. Traffic is usually heavy, so please use caution for this short stretch.*

16.2 *On your right is the Honeysuckle Hill B&B and Blacks Weaving Shop.*

On some days, you can stop and see the weavers at work.

16.3 *Turn right onto Maple Street, a scenic road with (despite its name) willow trees as well as stone walls and gentle hills.*

16.5 *Cross the railroad tracks with caution and pass Mill Pond to your left.*

16.6 *Turn left onto Cedar Street.*

16.9 *Turn left onto Willow Street.*

As the sign says, watch for horses crossing.

17.5 *Turn right onto Lombard Avenue, before the railroad tracks. Pass Barnstable Supply on your left (an interesting place to* browse); *the ball field and community building are on your right.*

17.6 *Turn left onto Route 149. The Whelden Library is on your left.*

17.8 *You're back at the Old Village Store and the tour's end.*

Bicycle Repair Services

Cove Cycle, 11 Enterprise Road, Hyannis, MA 508-771-6155

Pedaler Bicycle Shop, 3821 Route 28, Cotuit, MA 508-428-7396

The Bike Zone, 323 Barnstable Road, Hyannis, MA 508-775-3299

5

Barnstable and Yarmouthport

Distance: 12.6 miles
Terrain: Flat to gently rolling

One of the earliest established communities in the New World, Barnstable was founded in the mid-1600s. Consequently, this entire area along Cape Cod's central north shore is one of historic interest, its streets dotted with 200-year-old homes, historic meetinghouses, old graveyards, and weathered barns. Whether you choose to simply ride the back roads admiring the scenes of an earlier era or to stop at any of the numerous points of interest, the area is destined to provide a pleasant tour through the Cape's "quieter side."

Large tracts of coastal conservation land along various portions of the route provide a welcome glimpse of nature, where hiking trails, picnic areas, and the seashore lure you to abandon your bicycle and explore on foot for a while. The route is short enough that children can easily participate in the tour, and it allows ample time for everyone to explore the many side attractions.

The tour begins at Barnstable Village, not to be confused with the township of Barnstable, which includes seven villages (Barnstable, Centerville, Cotuit, Hyannis, Marstons Mills, Osterville, and West Barnstable), or with Barnstable County, which encompasses all of Cape Cod and has Barnstable Village as its seat.

Coming from "off-Cape," take the Sagamore Bridge onto Route 6 and proceed to exit 6. Turn left onto Route 132 toward Barnstable, then right onto Route 6A at the first intersection. For a more scenic approach you can get onto Route 6A just after crossing the bridge and proceed to the Route 132/Route 6A intersection. Barnstable Village is about 2.5 miles beyond the intersection. When you enter the village, park in the

5 • Barnstable and Yarmouthport

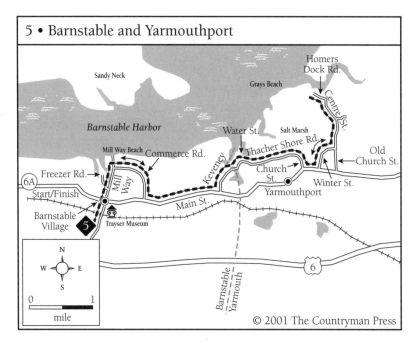

© 2001 The Countryman Press

courthouse parking lot just beyond the highly visible old courthouse on the hill to your right.

Either at the beginning or end of your tour, take time to explore the village of Barnstable. Small and easily negotiated, it boasts a thriving general store, good restaurants, a tavern with outside seating and draft beer and ale on tap, an ice cream shop, an antiques store, and other shops.

The courthouse on the hill, the present seat of government and law on Cape Cod, is distinguished by its four impressive stone pillars—at least they look like stone. On closer inspection you'll find them fabricated from wood. If you don't believe it, give them a tap and hear the hollow echo!

0.0 *Turn right out of the courthouse parking lot onto Route 6A.*

Originally an ancient Native American trail, this became a stage-coach route during colonial times. It was designated the King's Highway historic route in 1920, although the name was ill received by a population that prided itself on its staunch anti-monarchist heritage. It's now referred to as the King's Highway, Old King's Highway, or simply Route 6A.

0.1 Turn left onto Mill Way at the first set of lights.

For a short detour, continue instead straight up the steep hill. To your right will be the Trayser Museum, located in the Old Customs House, which served as the town post office until the 1950s. Open Tuesday through Friday during July and August, the museum has a variety of local artifacts—Native American relics; Victorian furnishings; early farm, carpentry, and fishing implements; a doll exhibit; and information on Barnstable's development during the era of sailing ships.

Across the street stands the Unitarian Church and Lothrop Hill Cemetery (the oldest in town). The large white building beside the church is the old schoolhouse, now a thrift store that's fun to browse through.

0.2 Pass by Cobb's Hill and West Cemetery, with its vaults built into the hillside.

0.4 Freezer Road is on your left.

You can take a 0.25-mile detour down Freezer Road and back. This short yet picturesque road is lined with marshes and old fishermen's cottages converted into pretty homes. The road is named for the condemned fish-freezer house, a relic of the days when a successful commercial fleet manned fish weirs in Barnstable Harbor.

0.6 Here you come to Barnstable Marina.

A number of boats here offer deep-sea-fishing day trips. A whale-watching boat offers trips twice daily in-season to view summering or migrating pilot, finback, and humpback whales from Mattacheese Wharf at the marina, where there's also a restaurant.

For a swim or a fine view of Barnstable Harbor, cross over the small bridge and continue on a short distance to the end at Mill Way Beach. As you cross the bridge, note the long inland marshes and creek to your right, home of numerous shorebirds throughout the year.

Barnstable Harbor is formed by Sandy Neck, a long, sandy peninsula visible in the distance that juts out into Cape Cod Bay. Once privately owned, the neck is now mostly town conservation land, its high dunes, extensive marshlands, and immense stretch of beach all protected. At the end of Sandy Neck lies the

Point, a small cluster of wooden houses where a summer community thrives as it has for generations.

The original lighthouse, now a private home, lies well back from the shoreline, evidence of the Cape's continually shifting sands. The harbor is dominated by 10-foot tides and an impressive current, which reaches 5 knots during midtide. What seems like an endless expanse of blue water at high tide becomes in many places a mere trickle between sand flats at low tide.

The shoreline is a fascinating natural display. In springtime, sea heather casts a dusky purple across the marsh grasses, while in the clear autumnal light they are green and golden. Seagulls, swallows, sandpipers, ducks, and herons fly overhead, bathe in the shallows, or bob on the gentle waves.

0.7 *Turn right onto Commerce Road. (If you visited Mill Way Beach, ride back 0.1 mile and turn left onto Commerce Road.)*

Commerce Road follows a continuous expanse of marshland and creeks, where migrating ducks, Canada geese, and great blue herons are frequent sights in fall.

1.5 *Turn left onto Route 6A.*

Many of the houses you pass along this stretch are among the oldest in the country. Some now serve as antiques shops, located either in the residence or in converted barns, and stopping for a look at their wares can be a pleasant addition to the tour.

2.3 *Here you come to Cummaquid Village Center.*

Cummaquid boasts no village sign, but its residents know where the town line lies. The tiny post office to your right is one of the Cape's smallest. A plaque to your left commemorates the Native American chief Iyanough, who "sold" the land to the early European settlers.

2.8 *Turn left onto Keveney Lane.*

This is a narrow paved road with some small hills along the way, culminating in a delightful downhill portion with breathtaking water views on both sides. Watch for patches of sand on either side of the single-lane bridge at the base of the hill.

3.2 *Cross a bridge straddling a tidal creek.*

A barn in Barnstable

Pause for a terrific view across the extensive marshes and creeks and out to Cape Cod Bay. In spring, note the osprey nest on one of the many nesting platforms dotting the great marshes of Cape Cod. Cross over the bridge and note the saltwater tidal pond to your right. Anthony's Cummaquid Inn, a well-known restaurant, can be seen across the pond.

Beyond the bridge, the road curves sharply to your right. The property on your left, including the thatch-roofed barn, is the private residence of the owner of the Christmas Tree Shops. The roof was thatched by professionals brought over from England.

3.3 *Turn left onto Water Street.*

3.5 *Take the unmarked, dead-end dirt lane to your left for a close-up view of the waterfront. Return to Water Street.*

3.7 *Turn left onto Thacher Shore Road.*

Here the route winds along the shorefront and marshland, much of it part of Yarmouth Conservation land.

4.1 *A small footpath leads down along the marshes through conservation land.*

4.3 Note the house on your right, beautifully landscaped with its lily-filled pond.

Spring is especially colorful at this spot, with multiflora roses heaped along a stone wall and masses of daisies, irises, and lupines spread across the field. Beyond the trees on your left is an unusually large barn, a relic of the Cape's early farming years.

4.5 Turn right onto Church Street.

To your right you'll see the Old Strawberry Hill Meetinghouse of the First Universalist Society, built in 1836 and now serving as a private residence.

4.6 Turn left onto Route 6A.

Directly across from you is the Colonial House Inn, overlooking the lovely Yarmouthport Village Green. Bicycling 0.1 mile west (to your right) as a slight detour offers several points of interest, including the village green, three historic houses, nature trails, and an unusual bookstore. The Thacher House, built in 1680, is one of the Cape's oldest, while the Winslow Crocker House, right next door, is a fine example of Colonial architecture. Portions of the Captain Bangs Hallet House, owned by the Historical Society of Old Yarmouth, date from 1740.

Nature trails, also maintained by the historical society and located behind the post office, offer excellent woodland hiking. Slightly farther along Route 6A brings you to Parnassus Bookstore, a true booklover's trove, with an eclectic assortment of literature piled high on shelves in this Old World–style shop.

4.7 Pass the Yarmouthport Village Store on your left.

4.9 Turn left onto Winter Street.

5.3 Pass a large graveyard on your left.

5.4 Turn left onto Centre Street.

5.8 Note the two lovely old houses on either side of the road, both with large, well-preserved barns.

5.9 Turn left onto Homers Dock Road.

You'll see a sign leading to Grays Beach. Here the road passes through town conservation land on both sides. There are two hiking trails here, one opposite Alms House Road, the other just before the Grays Beach parking lot on your left.

6.3 Reach Grays Beach, where a grassy picnic area with tables, shelter, and bathroom facilities lies beside the parking lot.

The view here is spectacular—sand dunes, tidal flats, marsh and creek, a small beach, and Sandy Neck Point seen far in the distance. Thick *Rosa rugosa,* its sweet-scented flowers blooming pink and white in early summer, line the marsh edge. Beyond, feathery marsh reeds wave like delicate flags above the cattails, and the air is filled with the calls of seagulls and red-winged blackbirds.

If you can, take the time to walk the 1,000-foot boardwalk out over marsh and water, following the course of Chase Garden Creek. You might catch sight of a marsh hawk gliding overhead, ducks floating at water's edge, or an osprey in its nest atop the pole in the marsh.

Return to Barnstable Village the same way in reverse, with the possible exception of continuing straight up Route 6A rather than taking the Thacher Shore Road. This offers you a chance to pass through Old Yarmouthport Center with its host of antiques shops, restaurants, historic houses, and the renowned Hallet's, a general store with an old-fashioned soda fountain. While this return route will also save you some time, be aware that bicycling Route 6A, especially in summer with the abundance of traffic, can be anything but relaxing.

Bicycle Repair Services

Idle Times Bike Shop, Route 134, South Dennis, MA 508-760-4515

The Bike Zone, 323 Barnstable Road, Hyannis, MA 508-775-3299

Yarmouth Bicycle, 63 Whites Path, South Yarmouth, MA 508-394-8941

6
Marstons Mills, Mashpee, and Cotuit

Distance: 19.0 miles
Terrain: Mostly flat, some gently rolling hills; protected exposure

Over the last two centuries, the Cape's largely undeveloped interior has faced the growing demand of city dwellers for second homes—for summer stays or retirement homes—golf courses, and resorts. The open spaces within Cape towns were prime sites for watersheds, golf courses, new schools, and parks.

Still, Marstons Mills and Cotuit preserved their village centers, the keys to their identities. The exception is Mashpee, which moved its police and fire stations, school, and library to a newly created village center off Routes 151 and Route 28 in the 1990s.

The change reflects Mashpee's dual identity as the historic home of the Cape's Wampanoag tribe and as a growing resort town.

Through a 3-day annual powwow in early July, the Mashpee Wampanoags still celebrate their culture with dancing, music, and food, such as the traditional clambake. The tribe did not celebrate the town's 125th anniversary in 1994, however. The Mashpee tribe is still fighting for federal recognition like that given to the Wampanoags of Gay Head on Martha's Vineyard. Mashpee's 1,500 members lost a 1978 lawsuit that claimed much of the land in Mashpee as their ancestral home. In 1638, missionary Richard Bourne of Sandwich convinced the Wampanoags of Mashpee to register their titles to their lands with the colonial court when he realized that colonists were buying up their entire homeland. Later, the colonial government set aside about 10,500 acres for the Native Americans and banned any land sales to colonists.

After decades of complaints, resident Wampanoags won some self-government by 1834. Many of the Cape's remaining Wampanoags tend-

6 • Marstons Mills, Mashpee, and Cotuit

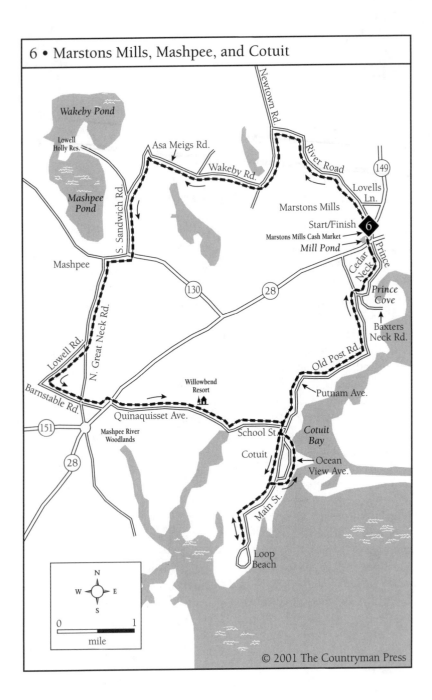

Wakeby Pond

Lowell
Holly Res.

Asa Meigs Rd.

Wakeby Rd.

Newtown Rd.

River Road

149

Lovells
Ln.

Marstons Mills

*Mashpee
Pond*

S. Sandwich Rd.

Start/Finish

6

Marstons Mills Cash Market

Mill Pond

Cedar Neck

Prince

Mashpee

130

28

*Prince
Cove*

Baxters
Neck Rd.

Lowell Rd.

N. Great Neck Rd.

Old Post Rd.

Willowbend
Resort

Putnam Ave.

Barnstable Rd.

151

Quinaquisset Ave.

Mashpee River
Woodlands

School St.

*Cotuit
Bay*

28

Cotuit

Ocean
View Ave.

Main St.

Loop
Beach

N
W E
S

0   1
mile

© 2001 The Countryman Press

ed to settle on tribal lands that also became a popular destination for hunters and anglers such as Daniel Webster and President Grover Cleveland.

The Native Americans' land, held in common, lost its protection in 1842, when the land was distributed, 60 acres per resident. Over the Wampanoags' objections, the state created the town of Mashpee in 1870.

Today Marstons Mills, Mashpee, and Cotuit offer a diverse cross-section of Cape Cod life. Together they hold an interesting mix of people, as well as woodlands, working cranberry bogs, lovely freshwater ponds, and access to the warm waters of Nantucket Sound on the south side of the Cape.

This tour begins at the Marstons Mills Cash Market on Route 149, near its intersection with Route 28.

0.0 *From the parking lot, go behind the market along River Road.*

This Barnstable village was named for Benjamin Marston, who ran a fulling mill here on the Marstons Mill River. Fulling mills were used to increase the weight and bulk of woolen cloth by repeated beating and pressing.

0.1 *Pass the Marstons Mills Post Office on your right.*

0.4 *Lovells Lane enters from your right. Veer left here, continuing on River Road.*

1.3 *You'll see working cranberry bogs on your right, and a large cranberry bog 0.3 mile from here on your left.*

2.1 *Turn left onto Newtown Road.*

This is the road to Newtown, another part of Barnstable with large working cranberry bogs.

2.2 *You come to the Long Pond Conservation Area, and more cranberry bogs will appear shortly on your left.*

Prize tomatoes and peppers come from the techniques employed in the community garden plots here. This area also has playing fields and a walking trail.

2.9 *Turn right onto Wakeby Road.*

3.8 *You cross the Mashpee town line here. Soon after, Wakeby Road merges with Asa Meigs Road, entering from your right.*

4.4 *Turn right onto Cotuit Road, then immediately turn left onto South Sandwich Road, a wooded section with newer homes.*

5.0 *Cross the Mashpee town line again.*

Near the line is an unmarked road to the Lowell Holly Reservation on a neck of land that separates Mashpee and Wakeby Ponds.

When he died in 1943, Harvard University president Abbott Lawrence Lowell donated this 130-acre site to the state for use as a nature reservation. The landscaping—native American holly, beech, red maple, and mountain laurel—was done by Lowell himself. The reservation area offers picnic areas and nature trails.

5.9 *Turn right onto Route 130 for a short distance. This is a busy road, so please use caution.*

This is the historic heart of Mashpee. Just ahead is the site of the annual powwow of the Wampanoag Nation. The state boat ramp on your right leads to Mashpee Pond.

6.2 *At the triangular intersection, turn left onto North Great Neck Road.*

You pass a country store on your right, the Mashpee Wampanoag Indian Museum, and the Mashpee Town Hall.

7.3 *Turn right at the fork onto Lowell Road.*

8.0 *Lowell Road passes Hay Road, an unmarked dirt road.*

You will get just a glimpse of the greens of the Quashnet Valley Golf Club.

8.1 *Turn left onto Barnstable Road (unmarked when we last saw it).*

Former president George Bush traveled this road on his last visit here, and a red, white, and blue line bisected the pavement.

8.4 *Mashpee Middle School is on your right.*

8.7 *Cross Great Neck Road at the stop sign and ignore the* DO NOT ENTER *sign as you enter a little-used leg of the Barnstable– Falmouth Road.*

9.4 *Turn left onto Route 28 for less than 0.1 mile. Then take a right onto Quinaquisset Avenue.*

Be careful. Route 28 is heavily traveled by speeding cars and their often-frustrated drivers.

9.6 *On your right is the entrance to the Mashpee River Wood-lands.*

Stop here for an unforgettable walk along dirt roads and easy trails. This 10-mile route follows the Mashpee River to South Cape Beach on Nantucket Sound. It is a link in a cross-Cape trail, part of a Cape Cod Pathways project to create a network of such walking trails throughout the Cape's 15 towns.

At the trail's start, you'll cross the river on old Route 28, little more than a cartpath. As you walk along you'll encounter former cranberry bogs and aqueducts for irrigation, salt marshes, prime warbler habitat, and spectacular views of the Mashpee River. Daniel Webster fished for trout in the Mashpee River in 1825 as he rehearsed his speech for the dedication of the Bunker Hill Monument.

10.6 *Pass the main entrance to the imposing Willowbend Resort.*

This resort was revived in the early 1990s by Paul Firestone of Reebok fame. Jimmy Connors and Bjorn Borg battled here in tennis tournaments. Greg Norman and Bobby Orr are among the sports legends who play here in charity golf tournaments.

11.0 *Cross the bridge when you come to it, looking over the upper reaches of Popponesset Bay. (This bridge is under repair and closed through the summer of 2001.)*

The road changes to School Street as you enter the village of Cotuit in the town of Barnstable.

11.5 *Enjoy this road's wonderful variety of architecture, such as "Twin Peaks," the house on your right. Pass the Cotuit High Ground Golf Club.*

12.0 *Enter the center of Cotuit and turn right onto Main Street.*

The Kettle-Ho restaurant, on your left before turning onto Main Street, is the center of village life, the place to be seen—and to be heard on topics of the day. After turning onto Main Street, you'll see Cotuit Bay on your left filled with the boats that harbor there in season.

12.5 *The Dottridge Homestead—home of the Historical Society of Santuit and Cotuit—is on your left.*

The homestead's furnishings date back to the era of 1800 to 1850.

The society's museum is in back of the homestead.

13.2 *Tall reeds of salt marshes line both sides of the road.*

13.4 *See how many swans are swimming in Rusty Marsh Pond on your left.*

To your right is a handful of large, imposing estates.

13.7 *You've arrived at the public beach, a popular spot in season, where the public road ends. Beyond are summer places and estates. Reverse direction and retrace your route along Main Street, heading north.*

14.6 *Turn right onto Ocean View Avenue.*

This section passes some of the Cape's oldest and loveliest homes.

15.1 *Turn right to rejoin Main Street.*

15.7 *Turn right onto Putnam Avenue.*

First you pass the Cotuit Grocery and then the Cotuit Pizza Factory, good places to refuel.

16.0 *Lowell Avenue enters on your left.*

The road leads to the ball park where the Cotuit Kettleers play in the Cape Amateur League; watching their games is a great summer pastime.

16.1 *Turn right onto Old Post Road.*

After your turn, you'll pass a cemetery on your left. This road goes along the shore of Cotuit Bay. You can see another harbor, full of boats, off to your right.

17.9 *Turn right onto Baxters Neck Road, then left onto Cedar Neck Road, which becomes Prince Avenue.*

Baxters Neck was the site of Camp Can-Do-It during World War II, a camp run by the Army Corps of Engineers for training operators of amphibious landing craft.

18.4 *Pass Prince Cove Marina, a small working boatyard.*

Prince Marston owned a brick house near the cove in the 1790s.

18.9 *Using caution, go straight across Route 28 onto Route 149.*

On your right is the preserved site of a 1689 fulling mill, one of the earliest known industrial sites in Massachusetts. Later a gristmill used this portion of the Marstons River, and in the 1940s a hydroelectric plant was powered by the stream.

Across Route 28, on your left, look to see if swans are gracing the waters or banks of picturesque Mill Pond. The pond, the herring run, and the space on the Route 28 corners were all donated to the town for open space in 1992.

19.0 **Finish at the Marstons Mills Cash Market, where your tour began.**

Bicycle Repair Services

Cove Cycle, 11 Enterprise Road, Hyannis, MA 508-771-6155

Pedaler Bicycle Shop, 3821 Route 28, Cotuit, MA 508-428-7396

The Bike Zone, 323 Barnstable Road, Hyannis, MA 508-775-3299

7
Centerville and Osterville

Distance: *13.5 miles*
Terrain: *Flat; sheltered*

The roads and elegant sea captains' houses along this route are reminders of the days when Centerville and Osterville were thriving centers of commerce and village life, visited by stagecoaches and trains.

In the 19th century, when 104 ship's captains called Centerville home, they added more than 50 houses and brought a cosmopolitan flair to the village.

Abolitionists brought runaway slaves here on the Underground Railroad. Centerville was home to the inventor of Technicolor and hosted the wedding of Caroline Kennedy.

Now public bathing beaches, golf courses, and summer houses stand in place of the wharves, piers, saltworks, and shipyards along the shores of the Sound and Centerville River, but the world still comes to Centerville and Osterville.

The tour begins on Main Street in Centerville, by the South Congregational Church and the 1856 Country Store. On weekends, park in the recreation building lot, across from the store and church.

0.0 **Turn right onto Main Street and head south. At the stoplight, turn right onto South Main Street.**

This road is usually quite busy, so feel free to use the sidewalk—giving the right of way to pedestrians, as always.

Turn left to find the Four Seas, a famous sandwich and ice cream shop. Even the Kennedy clan runs a tab here. If you can, save this treat for the end of your tour.

The Georgian-style mansion at the corner of Main and South Main Streets is home to the Eastern College Athletic Conference.

7 • Centerville and Osterville

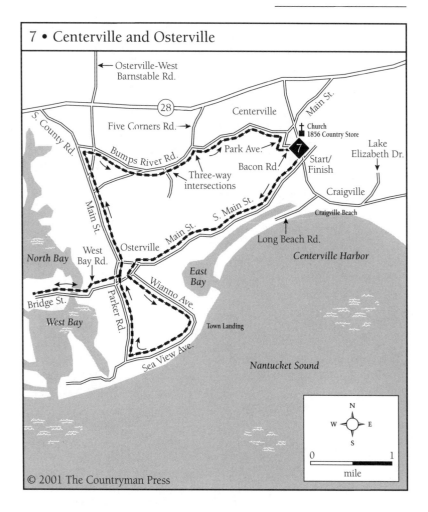

Osterville-West Barnstable Rd.

28

Centerville

Main St.

Five Corners Rd.

Church
1856 Country Store

Lake Elizabeth Dr.

S. County Rd.

Bumps River Rd.

Park Ave.

Bacon Rd.

7

Start/ Finish

Three-way intersections

Craigville

S. Main St.

Craigville Beach

Main St.

Main St.

Long Beach Rd.

Centerville Harbor

West Bay Rd.

Osterville

North Bay

East Bay

Parker Rd.

Wianno Ave.

Bridge St.

West Bay

Town Landing

Sea View Ave.

Nantucket Sound

N
W   E
S

0   1
mile

© 2001 The Countryman Press

1.0 *To your left, the Bumps River winds out to the Centerville River; some lovely homes sit above the river.*

2.5 *Turn left onto West Bay Road, then quickly left onto Wianno Avenue.*

You are now in Osterville Village. You'll pass a grocery store and two restaurants. Wianno Avenue was once a good straight run for winter sleigh racing. The Wianno neighborhood was named after Yanno, also known as Iyanough, a Native American sachem who lived in the 1600s.

3.6 *Wianno Avenue ends by the water at a town landing. Turn right here onto Sea View Avenue.*

You'll get a nice view of Nantucket Sound and some truly spectacular homes.

3.8 *The Wianno Club is to your left.*

This former pastureland was bought between 1863 and 1870 by Boston and New York investors. They developed a hotel, named the Cotachest House for the land's original Native American owner. The hotel burned in 1866 and was replaced by the building that later became this club. The club brought summer visitors, but their carpenters also stayed and raised their families here.

Abolitionist William Lloyd Garrison was one of the first to build a summer house here in Osterville. Both he and local Russell Marstons brought escaped slaves north to Cape Cod on the Underground Railroad.

4.6 *Turn right onto Parker Road.*

5.0 *Wianno Golf Club is on your left.*

5.6 *Turn left onto West Bay Road.*

This road leads to the drawbridge between West Bay and North Bay, two inlets that surround the Osterville islands. You'll pass the Osterville Historical Society and more evidence of the Wianno "Gold Club." Osterville has attracted old wealth such as DuPonts and new wealth such as William Koch of America's Cup fame.

5.9 *Turn left on Bridge Street and follow the road's turns. The drawbridge is straight ahead. Go over the drawbridge and ride onto Little Island, heading toward the exclusive and very private Oyster Harbors.*

On Bridge Street see the Wianno Yacht Club and one of Osterville's protected harbors on your left.

7.0 *The public road ends at the guarded entrance to Oyster Harbors. Enjoy your free view of the water and tidal marsh that some pay millions to enjoy. Reverse your direction and return toward Osterville.*

The 1856 Country Store in Centerville

7.9 Cross the drawbridge.

If you have time, stop at the parking lot to your right, just past the Wianno Yacht Club, and watch the boats in the harbor.

8.1 Back at West Bay Road, turn left to find Crosby's Boat Yard, famous for the creation of the Crosby catboat—a fisherman's workhorse in the 1840s—and for its years of maritime service.

The snack bar is open in summer, and there's a telephone and a view of Nauticus Marina, owned by William Koch.

8.3 Return to Bridge Street intersection and go straight on West Bay Road.

8.6 Turn left onto Parker Road and follow it to Main Street, past a cluster of houses built in the 1700s.

8.8 Turn left onto Main Street, heading out of town.

Or, for a side trip, turn right to stroll by the shops and stores along Main Street.

10.2 Turn right onto Bumps River Road.

This is a quiet stretch of road through the late-developed interior of the village. The road runs by the river named after Samuel Bumpas, a farmer here in the 1700s.

10.4 Cross the Osterville–West Barnstable Road.

Pass Cape Cod Academy on your right and Osterville Elementary School on your left.

11.3 At this three-way intersection, swing to your right to the stop sign and turn left to continue on Bumps River Road.

You'll soon pass the Skunknet River Wildlife Sanctuary, owned by the Massachusetts Audubon Society and open for exploration.

11.8 Pass Old Mill Road. Turn right to stay on Bumps River Road. The road to your left becomes Five Corners Road.

12.3 On your left is a very pretty pond, often home to swans.

12.7 A large cranberry bog is to your left.

13.1 Turn right onto Park Avenue and you're back in the long-settled part of Centerville.

13.3 Turn left onto Bacon Road.

This road was named after Reverend Elisha Bacon, a Congregational minister who had a private school here in 1852.

13.5 The tour ends back at Main Street in Centerville.

If you still feel like biking, continue through the stoplight and go 0.3 mile for a visit to Craigville Beach, a popular hangout among college kids in the summer.

Just before the beach you can turn right onto Long Beach Road; Long Beach is a sand barrier between the Sound and the Centerville River. There are several marked and public ways to the water that cross the lawns of the beach houses there.

After Craigville Beach, turn left onto Lake Elizabeth Drive and climb to Craigville, a former Methodist campground, established in 1872. Now its main building is a conference center and the many gingerbread cottages are year-round or summer homes, opened for a magical evening on Illumination Night each summer.

Bicycle Repair Services

Cove Cycle, 11 Enterprise Road, Hyannis, MA 508-771-6155

Pedaler Bicycle Shop, 3821 Route 28, Cotuit, MA 508-428-7396

The Bike Zone, 323 Barnstable Road, Hyannis, MA 508-775-3299

8
South Dennis to Chapin Beach

Distance: 21.2 miles
Terrain: Flat, with one incline; sheltered

People in this part of the Cape have long used their imagination. The Native Americans had two stories about the creation of Scargo Lake and Scargo Hill, local landmarks. One story goes that squaws using clamshells dug a hole, later filled by spring rains, for the pet fish of Princess Scargo. The other story describes how the giant Maushop scooped out the hole, creating the hill on which he sat and smoked his pipe to make Cape Cod fog.

About 1776, John Sears of Dennis first figured out how to make salt from seawater by means of evaporation. Quivett Neck and most of Sesuit Neck were covered with saltworks at one time.

In 1816, Henry Hall, of the Nobscusset part of Dennis, noticed that wild cranberry vines near the shore thrived when covered by windblown sand. He transplanted cranberry vines and re-created the natural conditions of flooding and sanding, which helped to cut down weeds and re-root vines; Hall's techniques are still used today. In 1820 he shipped 30 barrels of cranberries for sale off-Cape, starting a major Cape cash crop and a rush by other landowners to create their own cranberry barrens. Inventive in its own way, the first tax on cranberry lands was levied on Mr. Hall.

This tour starts on the ridge and descends to the fertile coastal plains of Sesuit, Quivett, and Nobscusset.

Park at the Market Street Shopping Center just off Route 134. To reach the center, take Route 6 to exit 9. Turn south on Route 134. Turn right at the first stoplight into the shopping center; you'll see a Dunkin' Donuts and other stores. Start at the stop sign, facing Route 134.

8 • South Dennis to Chapin Beach

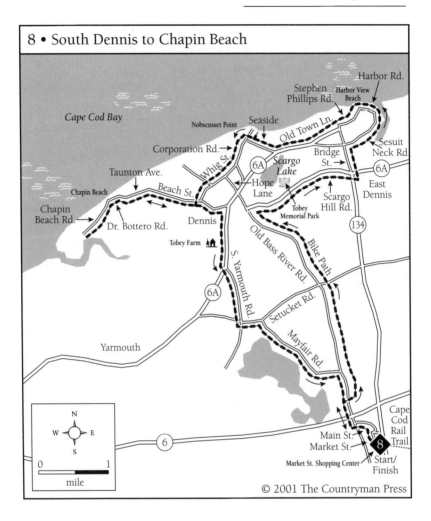

© 2001 The Countryman Press

0.0 *Turn left on Market Street, going out the side of the shopping center parking lot.*

0.1 *Turn left sharply onto Main Street.*

In 0.2 mile you'll see a sign with the words ENTERING SOUTH DEN-NIS HISTORIC DISTRICT.

0.6 *Turn right onto Old Bass River Road.*

At the corner is an old house with a white picket fence, the first of a stretch of elegant houses with stone walls. Pass the Red Cottage Store, a neighborhood meeting place, on your right.

1.0 Cross over Route 6. A bike path begins on your right.

You now enter a densely populated area, built up in the building boom of the 1960s and 1970s.

2.7 Cross Setucket Road.

3.7 Pass the Dennis Highlands Golf Course on your left.

Just beyond is a round water tank on your right.

4.1 Start descending Scargo Hill.

The hill is steep with some curves, so check your brakes and use caution.

4.3 Take a sharp right onto Scargo Hill Road.

Watch closely for this turn—you'll still be zooming downhill.

4.8 Tobey Memorial Park is to your left, with the Scargo Hill Tower and its sweeping view of Cape Cod Bay. The entrance to the park is a steep uphill, so relax and walk your bike.

The stone tower was given to the town in 1929 as a memorial to the Tobey family, who settled in Dennis in 1678. After you climb the tower's circular stairs, look to your left and you'll see the power-plant tower in Sandwich, as well as the headlands of Plymouth and all of Sandy Neck. Scargo Lake is straight ahead. Looking to your right, you can see the curve of the Outer Cape as it arches toward Provincetown.

5.0 Turn left onto Scargo Hill Road after leaving the park.

Continue downhill. The road levels off and passes through a scenic section of Dennis before reaching Route 6A, the old King's Highway.

5.2 On your left is the entrance to Princess Beach, a great family beach at the end of a 0.2-mile long dirt road.

There are stairs to the beach, a shelter overlooking the lake and latrines, but no drinking water.

6.3 Turn right onto Route 6A.

Use caution here. This road is heavily traveled. You'll pass stores, a motel, and, on your left, Grumpy's Breakfast and Lunch.

6.5 *Turn left onto Bridge Street. Head north toward Cape Cod Bay.*

As you approach the intersection of Route 134 and Bridge Street, you'll pass several antiques shops. The Captain Judah Paddock House, a local landmark, is at the corner.

6.7 *On your right is the Marshside Restaurant, which overlooks beautiful salt marshes and tidal streams and is a lovely place for lunch and bird-watching.*

6.9 *Turn right onto Sesuit Neck Road.*

Head toward Sesuit Harbor along this winding road. You'll pass many older homes that preserve the historic Cape architecture as well as the natural landscaping of cedar trees, honeysuckle, lilacs, and daylilies.

7.5 *Pass the Shiverick Memorial on your right. The town's marina is just after the memorial, also on your right. The road becomes Harbor Road as it curves to your left along the eastern shore of Sesuit Neck.*

The memorial describes the old Shiverick Shipyard, where many large schooners and clipper ships were built during the 1800s. Among them were the schooners *Watson Baker, J. K. Baker, Searsville*, and *Westwind*, as well as the speedy *Revenue, Belle of the West*, and *Kit Carson*.

7.7 *Pass the Dennis Yacht Club.*

You'll start to see sandy dunes and large homes with water views.

7.8 *Pass Harborview Beach and veer left on Stephen Phillips Road. You'll soon see a cranberry bog on the right.*

A stone jetty protects a stretch of water that leads to the Dennis Yacht Club and the boatyard, large tidal marshes, and water views. Stop for a swim if you have time.

8.4 *Turn left onto Bridge Street.*

8.5 *Turn right onto Old Town Lane.*

The narrow road is a trip into another era, with split-rail fences along the road, views to the ocean, groomed hedges, cedar-lined streets, and stone walls.

Cove Road landing on the Bass River is a good place to land fish or boats.

8.9 *Turn right onto Sesuit Neck Road.*

9.2 *Turn right onto Route 6A.*

Pass a pottery shop on your left and follow the curving road to your left. Scargo Lake and its town landing, topped by Scargo Tower, are also to the left.

9.5 *Turn right onto Seaside Avenue.*

You're entering the part of Dennis called Nobscusset, named after the Native Americans who once lived here. The Cape's first salt-works, the first cultivated cranberry bog, and the elegant Nobscusset Hotel were part of this neighborhood's past.

9.9 *Turn right onto Corporation Road, which takes you to Corporation Beach. After visiting the beach, retrace your path on Corporation Road.*

This beach is a nice place to walk, fly kites, or watch windsurfers. Both the road and beach were named after the Nobscusset Point Pier Corporation, established in 1814 by Henry Hall and others.

10.3 *Pass the Seaside Avenue intersection to your left and enjoy the road, shaded by overhanging trees.*

10.7 *Turn right onto Whig Street.*

11.0 *Turn left at Hope Lane, and in 0.2 miles turn left at the mailboxes to find the Cape Museum of Fine Arts.*

The museum opened in 1985 with a growing collection of works by Cape painters from the 1900s to the present. The museum shares the site with the Cape Playhouse, a wonderful summer theater, and the Cape Cinema, known for its Rockwell Kent ceiling mural and eclectic films.

11.4 *Return to Whig Street and turn left.*

As you approach Whig Street, look straight ahead of you. There's an excellent example of a three-quarter Cape, complete with assorted additions.

11.5 *Continue across Nobscusset Road.*

To your left at Nobscusset Road is the Josiah Dennis Manse, built in 1736. The town was named after the Reverend Josiah Dennis, who lived here until his death in 1763. Dennis was first settled in

1639 as part of Yarmouth but didn't become a town until it split from Yarmouth in 1793.

Now the restored house, along with the town's oldest existing schoolhouse, is a historical center.

11.8 *Turn right onto Beach Street.*

12.6 *Turn left at the fork onto Taunton Avenue, nearing Cape Cod Bay.*

This neighborhood is nicknamed "Little Taunton" or "Little Italy" because of five families from Taunton and, later, several Italian families who settled here starting in the 1920s.

13.1 *Turn left onto Dr. Bottero Road.*

Numerous summer cottages are packed into the dunes along this stretch of your route.

13.3 *The road you're on becomes Chapin Beach Road. Watch for sand patches on the road.*

Enjoy the whole sweep of the Dennis barrier beach. There's a salt marsh to your left and sand dunes and the beach to your right.

This beach was a gift to the town by real-estate broker George Halliday Chapin shortly after World War II. Before that, the beach was known as Black Flats because of the sand's color.

At the end of the beach and to your left is Aquacultural Research Corporation, long a source of seed clams for Cape waters and clamshells for Cape driveways.

13.8 *After checking out Chapin Memorial Beach, retrace your steps to Dr. Bottero Road.*

14.5 *Turn right onto Taunton Avenue.*

15.0 *Turn right onto Beach Street.*

15.7 *Go past Whig Street on your left. At stop sign, turn left.*

16.2 *Turn right onto Route 6A, again using caution.*

Explore the local gift and antiques shops, art gallery, bakery, and café, all within half a mile.

16.7 *Pass the Tobey Farm, which offers fresh produce in the summer and cider and pumpkins in the fall.*

17.0 Turn left onto South Yarmouth Road.

As the name implies, you'll soon cross into Yarmouth.

17.9 Turn left onto Setucket Road. There's a sidewalk on your left.

18.2 Cross back into Dennis. Turn right onto Mayfair Road.

This is a densely populated road with gentle hills.

19.7 Turn right onto Old Bass River Road. There's a bike path on your left.

20.3 Cross over the Mid-Cape Highway.

20.7 Take a sharp left onto Main Street. Loop around toward Market Street.

21.2 Turn right onto Market Street. Swing around to the shopping center and return to the start of your tour.

Bicycle Repair Services

Barbara's Bike, 430 Route 134, South Dennis, MA 508-760-4723

Idle Times Bike Shop, Route 134, South Dennis, MA 508-760-4515

THE LOWER CAPE

9 • Brewster, Harwich, and Nickerson State Park

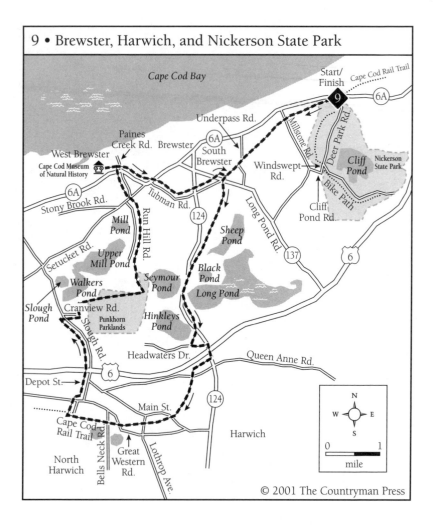

Cape Cod Bay

Start/
Finish

Cape Cod Rail Trail

6A

Underpass Rd.

Paines
Creek Rd. Brewster

South
Brewster

6A

Millstone Rd.

Deer Park Rd.

West Brewster

Cape Cod Museum
of Natural History

Windswept
Rd.

Cliff
Pond

Nickerson
State Park

Tubman Rd.

124

Bike Path

Cliff
Pond Rd.

6A

Stony Brook Rd.

Setucket Rd.

Run Hill Rd.

Mill
Pond

Long Pond Rd.

Sheep
Pond

Upper
Mill Pond

Black
Pond

137

6

Walkers
Pond

Seymour
Pond

Long Pond

Slough
Pond

Cranview Rd.

Punkhorn
Parklands

Hinkleys
Pond

Slough Rd.

Headwaters Dr.

Queen Anne Rd.

Depot St.

6

124

N
W   E
S

Main St.

124

Harwich

0   1
mile

Cape Cod
Rail Trail

Bells Neck Rd.

North
Harwich

Great
Western
Rd.

Lothrop Ave.

© 2001 The Countryman Press

9
Brewster, Harwich, and Nickerson State Park

Distance: *20.7 miles*
Terrain: *Some moderate hills; mostly sheltered*

This trail through Brewster, the sea captains' town, also takes you through a slice of Harwich's cranberry bogs and off-road through the Punkhorn Parklands. It starts and finishes at Nickerson State Park, the state's oldest, largest, and most popular state park.

Originally, the park was the turn-of-the-century hunting resort of Roland C. Nickerson, a builder of railroads in the West. His parents had amassed the woodlot and ponds in the late 1800s that became their son's Bungalow Estate. Roland imported elk, bear, and other prey into these woods for his hunting guests, including President Grover Cleveland.

In 1934, Roland's widow and his daughter donated 1,750 acres of the hunting grounds as a state park. The red-roofed family mansion and carriage house, overlooking the King's Highway (Route 6A) and Cape Cod Bay, is now the Ocean Edge Resort and Golf Club.

The 2,000-acre park holds 400 campsites (for reservations contact Roland C. Nickerson State Park, Route 6A, Brewster, MA 02631, 508-896-3491), four ponds stocked with rainbow and brown trout, and a mile of waterfront on Cape Cod Bay. Diagonally across town, the Punkhorn Parklands comprises more than 835 acres of deep woods between Brewster, Dennis, and Harwich, crisscrossed with old roads and paths to cranberry bogs and kettle ponds. The town acquired 600 acres of the inland woods in one push between 1985 and 1988. The conservation area now offers 45 miles of walking and off-road bicycling trails. Maps of the Punkhorn are available in the visitors center in the Brewster Town Hall, or by mail (write: Conservation Commission, Brewster

Town Hall, Route 6A, Brewster, MA 02631, 508-897-3701). Such stretches of open space, preserved from the past, are part of what defines Brewster.

To savor the Brewster portion of Cape Cod Bay, go west on Route 6A less than 0.1 mile from the entrance to Nickerson State Park and turn right onto Crosby Lane. To your left is the "window on the bay," 90 acres of land and a mile of waterfront on Cape Cod Bay, added to the state park in 1987. You'll pass the Crosby Mansion, built in 1860 and now under restoration, on your way to the bay.

Beyond Crosby Lane, 0.3 mile on Route 6A, you'll find the Brewster Historical Society's Museum at Spruce Hill, a 25-acre parcel bought by the town of Brewster in 1985. The full Cape house, now the museum, was the 1840 homestead of the Keelers, the first Irish immigrants to settle in Brewster.

Beyond the house are trails through spruce trees, wildflowers, and a tupelo swamp to the dunes and beach on Cape Cod Bay. The walk is about a mile round-trip, a good warm-up or reward for a bike ride.

Park at Nickerson State Park, Brewster, to the right of the main entrance. To reach this park from Route 6, take exit 12 and turn toward Brewster on Route 6A. The state park is well marked, on your left, about 2 miles away. There's an alternate parking lot, west of the main entrance, near the seasonal Idle Times Bike Shop.

0.0 *Turn left (right from the alternate lot) onto the Cape Cod Rail Trail at the end of the parking lot.*

0.7 *Cross Millstone Road.*

This is a very busy road where cars usually travel fast.

2.2 *Cross Underpass Road.*

The shop here offers great sandwiches and picnic supplies. The road was named after a now-gone railroad underpass.

2.7 *Cross Long Pond Road (Route 137).*

4.6 *Cross Route 124. Seymour Pond is on your right and Black Pond on your left.*

You're now in the town of Harwich, the mother town of Brewster, which was Harwich's North Parish. This is a terrific spot for rest, a snack, or a water break.

4.7 *Cross Route 124 again.*

On your left is Long Pond, another scenic resting place, usually favored by a cooling breeze. This pond covers more than 700 acres in Brewster and Harwich.

5.1 *Cross Route 124 yet again.*

On your right, just before crossing Route 124, is the Pleasant Lake General Store, once a district school for South Brewster. This is your last chance for miles to stock up on drinks and supplies.

5.2 *The trail veers away from Route 124 between vast cranberry bogs and Hinkleys Pond, a beautiful but exposed ride.*

5.8 *By summer 2002, you will be able to cross Headwaters Drive to ride a new bicycle bridge across Route 6. Until then, turn left off the bike trail onto Headwaters Drive. Follow this road to Route 124.*

To your left are the redbrick buildings of Cape Cod Regional Technical High School, serving students from Barnstable to Provincetown. Its student-run café is a great bargain during the school year.

6.1 *Turn right onto Route 124 and cross Route 6.*

You'll pass a junkyard and antiques shop on your right, and highway exits on your left. Use caution here; the new bike bridge will eventually avoid this stretch of road.

6.4 *Pass two highway exit ramps and the parking lot for commuters who bus to Boston, and turn right onto the bike trail.*

6.9 *Cross Queen Anne Road.*

Since there's a King's Highway, it seems only fair that there be a Queen Anne Road, named in 1712 by Chatham in honor of the queen of England. The road stretches from Yarmouth to Chatham.

7.8 *Cruise around the rotary and through the tunnel under Main Street.*

The trail to the left runs nearly 3.5 miles through Harwich Center to end, for now, in the woods at the Chatham town line.

8.4 *Cross Lothrop Avenue.*

8.8 *Cross Great Western Road.*

To your right you'll see a large cranberry bog backed by "borrow" sites of sand; the sand is used to cover the cranberries to increase productivity. Soon you'll pass Bells Neck Road, a dirt road that runs between two reservoirs. Catch a last glimpse of the reservoirs' gleaming water as you cross the Herring River. You passed the river's mouth back at Hinkleys Pond, near Route 124.

9.6 *Turn right onto Depot Street, leaving the bike trail.*

The gray building on your left was a warehouse for processing and storing cranberries before they were shipped off-Cape by rail.

9.8 *At the corner, turn right onto Great Western Road. Turn left quickly back onto Depot Street.*

In Harwich, the road's name is Depot Street. As you travel into Brewster, the road's name changes to Slough Road.

10.5 *Enter Brewster on Slough Road.*

11.5 *Turn right onto Cranview Road, an entrance to the Punkhorn Parklands. Heading downhill, pass the bog and glimpse Elbow Pond to the right.*

"Find yourself, lost in the woods," says the town's guide to the Punkhorn. It's not hard to do on the 45 miles of trails in these 835 acres. The area was acquired by the town in the 1960s.

Punkhorn, probably meaning "rotten or spongy wood," was what snobby town dwellers called their country neighbors. Now city dwellers love to escape to the Punkhorn. Before the woods grew back, the land was a sheep commons. The rusted cars here were not dumped but brought to their sites to power the pumps that flooded the cranberry bogs.

11.7 *Turn left at the mailboxes onto Black Duck Cartway.*

On the left, a trail will lead to shady Walker's Pond.

12.2 *Archie's Cartway, one of the few marked roads, intersects from the left.*

The cartway leads to Capt. Daniel's Neck, between Walkers Pond and Upper Mill Pond.

12.5 *Turn left onto Westgate Road.*

This gravel road leads through more scrubby pine and oak woods,

A simple full Cape house with central door and chimney.

now a haven for many songbirds who need such undisturbed habitat.

12.9 *Veer left at fork.*

Visit Mill Pond landing for a look at a lovely pond and a place for picnicking, kayaking, and canoeing.

13.4 *Pass the parking lot on Run Hill Road on your way out of the Punkhorn.*

To the right, just past Red Maple Road, are more trails—to Calf Field and Tuckers Pond. Run Hill widens to a paved road and passes the town disposal area.

14.6 *Turn left onto Setucket Road.*

This scenic road was the main road between Dennis and Brewster and will lead you into the Stony Brook Valley.

Cruise down the steep hill to the Stony Brook Grist Mill and Museum and Herring Run on Mill Pond.

This lovely place was once known as Factory Town, thanks to its water-powered gristmill, tannery, and mills. The first gristmill was here before 1677. The present mill was built in 1873 on the foundations of old fulling and woolen mills. Factories here made overalls and ice cream, and the mill still grinds corn in summer. The town purchased the mill and mill site in 1940.

Another major attraction in late April and May is the Herring Run. From Paines Creek on the bay 1.5 miles downstream, the herring leap up ladders or steps, resting in deep pools before leaping again to reach their spawning grounds above the mill in Lower and Upper Mill Ponds and Walkers Pond.

Rights to the herring, valuable as commercial fertilizer and pet food, were once sold to the highest bidder. When fish stocks permit, residents net their own herring; the bony fish were locally prized for their roe, for smoking, and for garden fertilizer.

As you return to Run Hill Road, notice the house to your right, once a stagecoach stop when this road was the main route from Dennis.

14.9 Pass Run Hill Road and turn left onto Paines Creek Road.

This road parallels the descent of Stony Brook Valley to Paines Creek Marsh.

15.2 Turn left on Route 6A.

Cross the marsh, where circling and calling gulls in the spring signal the arrival of the herring.

15.5 On your right you'll find the Cape Cod Museum of Natural History.

The museum trails lead through the woods and marshes to Cape Cod Bay. For an affordable entry fee, you can enjoy excellent exhibits explaining the natural history and human history of what you see. (Write or call the museum: Route 6A, Brewster, MA 02631, 508-896-3867.)

15.6 Retrace your route along Route 6A, heading east.

This portion of Route 6A, all the way back to Nickerson State Park, has been nominated for the National Register of Historic Places. Enjoy the elegant homes, antiques shops, bed & breakfasts, and art galleries along the road. Café Alfresco is a good place for coffee, lunch, or a snack.

16.4 Pass Stony Brook Road and turn right onto Tubman Road.

Tubman Road is a nice shady ride, with old New England stone walls and lovely landscaping.

17.4 Cross Route 124—again!

17.9 Bear right onto Route 137.

18.0 Turn left onto the Cape Cod Rail Trail and return to Nickerson State Park, 2.7 miles away.

Maps available at the park office will help you explore the 7.5 miles of paved trails that cover the roller-coaster hills of the park. The Park Trail parallels the park road, from the main buildings at the park entrance through woods and around ponds for a round trip of 6 miles. The Ober Trail veers off to your right as the Park Trail leaves the main parking area. A middle trail leaves the Ober Trail, ending near the park store. A fourth trail runs between the middle trail and Ober Trail and passes along a cedar swamp. A fifth trail leaves the Park Trail and climbs to circle the jewel of Ruth Pond in the upper part of the park.

Bicycle Repair Services

Brewster Bike Shop, 442 Underpass Rd., Brewster, MA 508-896-8149

Dr. Gravity's Bike Shop, 564 Route 28, Harwichport, MA 508-430-0437

Harwichport Bike Co., 431 Route 28, Harwichport, MA 508-430-0200

Idle Times Bike Shop, Route 6A, Brewster, MA 508-896-9242

Monomoy Sail & Cycle, 275 Orleans Rd., N. Chatham, MA 508-945-0811

Orleans Cycle, 26 Main St., Orleans, MA 508-255-9115

Rail Trail Bikes & Blades, 302 Underpass Rd., Brewster, MA 508-896-8200

10
South Dennis and Harwich

Distance: *18.3 miles*
Terrain: *Flat; mostly sheltered*

In fewer than 20 miles, this trail covers 200 years of economic development on Cape Cod, traveling past working cranberry bogs, clusters of historic houses, summer neighborhoods, busy beaches, fishing piers, and cottages renovated into year-round homes.

The cranberry industry got its start in Dennis on Cape Cod Bay, but the industry's techniques were polished in the bogs near Pleasant Lake in Harwich.

The cranberries were freighted off-Cape by the railroad that made South Dennis, at the center of Dennis, into the town's largest village. The railroad still hauls freight to the lumberyard on Route 134. From there, the old railroad bed now carries bicyclists, walkers, skaters, and cross-country skiers on the Cape Cod Rail Trail, which extends into Wellfleet with ample stops in intervening towns.

In the 1880s, the railroad also brought tourists to the Cape to spend entire summers, spurring the creation of new colonies of cottages and waterfront hotels and resorts. Later the automobile shortened the trip, creating a market for motels and second homes.

Park at the Cape Cod Rail Trail parking lot off Route 134. To get there, take Route 6 to exit 9, then turn south onto Route 134. Pass through one stoplight, then move into the center lane. The bike trail parking lot is on your left, with two bike shops nearby.

0.0 Go out the rear of the parking lot onto the bike trail.

0.8 Cross Gages Way.

      Detour left along the paved sidewalk for 0.2 mile to inspect the

10 • South Dennis and Harwich

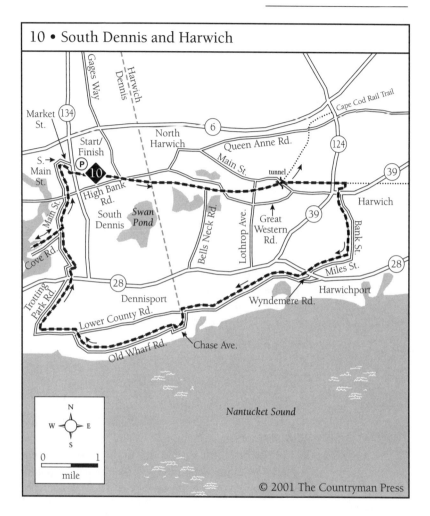

Market St. (134)

Gages Way

Harwich Dennis

Start/ Finish

S.→ Main St.

Main St.

North Harwich

(6)

Queen Anne Rd.

Main St.

tunnel

Cape Cod Rail Trail

(124)

(39)

High Bank Rd.

South Dennis

Swan Pond

Bells Neck Rd.

Lothrop Ave.

Great Western Rd.

(39)

Harwich

Bank St.

Cove Rd.

(28)

Trotting Park Rd.

Dennisport

Lower County Rd.

Miles St.

(28)

Harwichport

Wyndemere Rd.

Old Wharf Rd.

Chase Ave.

Nantucket Sound

N
W   E
S

0   1
mile

© 2001 The Countryman Press

Tony Kent Arena, practice ice for figure skaters Nancy Kerrigan and Paul Wylie and the home ice of the Scotvolds, who train and coach world-class skaters here.

0.9 *Cross Great Western Road.*

Use caution. This is a busy road through the industrial heart of Dennis. Its curves show its age; it dates far back as an interior road between Harwich Center, Weir Road, and Route 6A in Yarmouth.

1.5 Cross Depot Street in Harwich.

The street name recalls the days when this part of town was the rail hub of Dennis and Harwich. The big building to your left was a warehouse for the processing and storage of cranberries until they were shipped off-Cape.

Pass by a cranberry bog on your left and one on your right. Take in the view of Herring River on your right and, on your left, enjoy the easy chairs for a rest and a summary of the rail trail's history.

2.1 Cross Bells Neck Road.

This dirt road on your right leads to the surrounding town-owned conservation land located between two reservoirs. These waters are fishing grounds for perch, bass, and pickerel and swimming grounds for swans. If you take this detour, you'll find a nice resting place half a mile downhill to your right on the gravel road. Go a little beyond to reach a footbridge across the Herring River. This neck is named after John Bell, who owned much of this property in the 1600s.

2.4 Cross Great Western Road.

Admire the vast bog on your left. Notice the "borrow" sites for sand on the back hill. In winter, the sand is spread across the flooded bog to smother weeds and encourage branching of the cranberry vines.

2.9 Cross Lothrop Road.

The swordlike leaves of the yucca plant defend the trail entrance here. In summer, its blooms dangle like ornaments from its tall stalk. This perennial often guards driveways and boundaries on Cape Cod.

3.4 Go through a tunnel under Main Street to a rotary junction.

Veer right on the trail that leads through Harwich Center. This 3.4-mile-long trail now ends in the woods at the Harwich-Chatham line but eventually will extend into downtown Chatham.

4.2 Stop at Route 124 after riding past Island Pond and its namesake cemetery.

Cross Route 124 on foot and ride along Old Colony Road on the former railbed. You'll pass behind Town Hall, which fronts Main Street. There are bike racks here if you want to explore its shops and library.

4.4 *Turn right on Oak Street.*

To your left are the town's schools and, beyond that, the Cranberry Valley Golf Course and cranberry bogs. You'll pass Brooks Park, site of crafts fairs, concerts, and other town celebrations. This is the center of Harwich, incorporated in 1694 and named after a town in Essex, England, that was a departing port for many immigrants who settled here.

For a short detour through peaceful woods, follow the bike path 2.5 miles and return.

4.5 *Turn right onto Main Street (Route 39). Turn left immediately onto Bank Street, past Brooks Free Library.*

Now you're riding past Harwichport's stylish mansions, Queen Anne–style homes, and cranberry bogs.

5.6 *Turn right onto Miles Street. Cross South Street and approach busy Route 28 with caution.*

To your left is a shopping center with a convenience and a liquor store, telephones, a pizza parlor, and a pharmacy.

7.4 *Angle across Route 28 onto Wyndemere Road. Turn right onto Lower County Road.*

Pass scenic Allen Harbor. Detour left at any point to explore the many roads that lead to beaches on Nantucket Sound, all with great views.

9.0 *Turn left onto Pleasant Road. The beach is 0.2 mile away and restrooms are available in season. Return to Lower County Road and turn left.*

9.8 *Cross the Herring River, last viewed from the rail trail. Turn left onto Belmont Road.*

10.4 *Turn right onto Chase Avenue, entering the town of Dennis, then turn right onto Depot Street.*

10.8 *Turn left onto Old Wharf Road. Follow it past a series of beaches, campgrounds, cottages, and restaurants that, for many, defines summer on Cape Cod.*

Susan Milton

Pleasant Road Beach in Harwich on Nantucket Sound

Fishing remained a major industry along this coast for 75 years, from 1795 to the mid-1800s. Farther west, the Bass River was a destination for coasters transporting coal, grain, and lumber.

12.4 Turn left onto Lower County Road and cross the Swan Pond River.

13.1 Turn right onto Trotting Park Road.

Its straightaway reminds a rider of the racetrack located here in the late 1800s.

14.1 Cross Route 28.

You'll pass the Ezra Baker School on your right and then enter the South Dennis Historic District, a living example of the evolution of Cape houses from the 18th century to the present.

At the next corner, for example, the Jericho Museum was built in 1801 by Captain Theosophilus Baker. This home is one of Dennis's historical centers, now fully restored and furnished with antiques, cranberry equipment, a saltworks model, and an old-fashioned grocery store. Owners Elizabeth Reynard, author of *This Narrow Land*, and Dr. Virginia Gildersleeve, a president of Barnard College, bought the building in 1955 and named it the Jericho Museum because its walls were about to tumble down. They donated the restored building to the town in 1962.

14.3 Turn right, passing Center Street, to Main Street.

14.7 On your right, check the time on the clock of the South Congregational Church.

The church, built in 1835, holds a rosewood organ built in 1762 by the same craftsman who built an instrument for composer George Handel.

14.8 Turn left down Cove Road.

This is a bumpy road, first paved then gravel, that leads to a town landing. Cove Road is now home to stunning new houses, examples of the Cape's changing development. Few old Cape Codders built near the shores, knowing that natural forces could wreak havoc on buildings and farms. Now such waterfront views are prized by retirees and vacationers.

The town landing at the end overlooks Bass River and, on the far side, Yarmouth. Bass River, the largest stretch of inland water in the county, stretches from Nantucket Sound to Follins Pond.

15.5 From the town landing, retrace your route back to Main Street.

16.2 At Main Street, turn left.

You'll pass nice old Capes and half-Capes, a bog on your left with inviting benches, and the South Dennis Public Library.

16.8 Cross High Bank Road at the stop sign.

On your right is Liberty Hall, a town meeting place since 1844, when the building was moved to this site. The versatile structure has been a store, a furniture showroom, a doctor's office, a millinery store, a post office, and a stagecoach stop. Now Liberty Hall hosts village suppers and meetings and houses a summer thrift shop.

17.0 Pass Dennis Town Hall on your left.

For a break, stop at the town hall parking lot and take a walk to the Indian Lands. This conservation trail leads through upland and marshes to overlook the Bass River. In late May and early June, its pine woods are carpeted with lady's slippers.

17.2 Turn right onto South Main Street.

17.8 Turn right onto Market Street. Pass the post office and swing left, around the rail fence, through the shopping center, to the stoplight at Route 134.

18.0 Cross Route 134 and, on the far side, turn right onto the paved sidewalk.

This passes by Patriot's Square, with grocery, book, hardware, and clothing stores, as well as restaurants and movie theaters.

18.3 Turn left into the Cape Cod Rail Trail parking lot, where your tour began.

Bicycle Repair Services

Brewster Bike Shop, 442 Underpass Rd., Brewster, MA 508-896-8149

Dr. Gravity's Bike Shop, 564 Route 28, Harwichport, MA 508-430-0437

Harwichport Bike Co., 431 Route 28, Harwichport, MA 508-430-0200

Idle Times Bike Shop, Route 6A, Brewster, MA 508-896-9242

Monomoy Sail & Cycle, 275 Orleans Rd., N. Chatham, MA 508-945-0811

Rail Trail Bikes & Blades, 302 Underpass Rd., Brewster, MA 508-896-8200

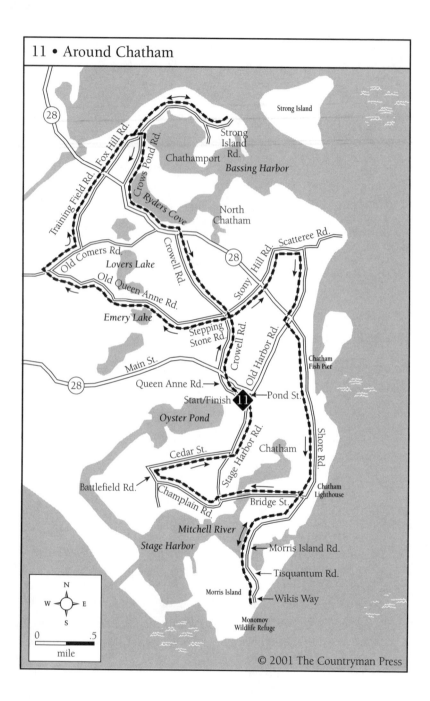

Strong Island

Strong Island Rd.

Bassing Harbor

Chathamport

Training Field Rd. Fox Hill Rd.

Crows Pond Rd.

Ryders Cove

North Chatham

28

Old Comers Rd.

Lovers Lake

Crowell Rd.

Scatteree Rd.

Stony Hill Rd.

Old Queen Anne Rd.

Emery Lake

Stepping Stone Rd.

Crowell Rd.

Old Harbor Rd.

Chatham Fish Pier

Main St.

28

Queen Anne Rd.

Start/Finish 11 Pond St.

Oyster Pond

Shore Rd.

Chatham

Cedar St.

Stage Harbor Rd.

Battlefield Rd.

Champlain Rd.

Bridge St.

Chatham Lighthouse

Mitchell River

Stage Harbor

Morris Island Rd.

Tisquantum Rd.

Morris Island

Wikis Way

Monomoy Wildlife Refuge

N
W   E
S

0   .5
mile

© 2001 The Countryman Press

11
Around Chatham

Distance: 17.3
Terrain: Hilly

Mariners unsure of their bearings used to look for the beacons shining from Chatham's shores—a single beacon for Monomoy Light, a twin beacon for the twin Chatham Lights, and three beacons for Nauset Light—to get an accurate fix on their position. Sometimes, however, they were fooled by the "mooncussers," men waving lanterns and causing ships to wreck on Chatham's treacherous shoals so they could steal their cargoes.

Easy to find by sea, Chatham is out of the way by land. The town, established in 1712, is to the southeast of Harwich and Orleans, on Cape Cod's outer elbow.

Over the years, the excellent fishing and hunting have drawn sportsmen to the duck blinds and camps on North Beach. Chatham has also long been known for its "highliners," expert fishermen who sail out of Chatham Harbor and Stage Harbor. In the 20th century, both the wealthy and the royal summered here to enjoy Chatham's beaches, ponds, and shopping. On a walk along Main Street you can find elegant clothing, exciting artwork, good coffee, and excellent food—from codcakes and steamers to haute cuisine.

This tour travels through the old and new, inland and seaside, of Chatham. Park at Oyster Pond near the end of Stage Harbor Road. If the parking spaces are full, go toward the church spire and rotary on Stage Harbor Road. Look for the sign for public parking on your right.

0.0 *Leave the Oyster Pond parking lot at the big boulder, a monument to Korean and Vietnam War veterans. Turn left immediately onto Pond Street.*

0.3 Turn left onto Queen Anne Road.

Notice the bow roof on the guest house on your right.

0.4 At the stoplight on Route 28, use care in crossing straight across onto Crowell Road, past the Christian Science church on your right.

You'll pass a cemetery and the Chatham Drama Guild on your right; shops, a bakery, and a bike-and-skate shop on your left.

1.0 Turn left onto Stepping Stone Road and climb uphill.

1.4 Turn right onto Old Queen Anne Road.

You can ride on the sidewalk on your right, if you wish. On this hilly ride, pass Emery Lake on your left and Lovers Lake on your right. The lovers are unknown, but the former lake is named after the Reverend Stephen Emery, Chatham's third minister.

2.0 Pass George Ryder Road on your left.

The Chatham Old Burying Ground, split in two by Old Queen Anne Road, holds the graves of the Searses, Nickersons, Crowells, and Ryders who developed the town. The older, hilly section holds a large Victorian obelisk, the Sears Memorial, and other well-marked stones from the 1760s. A historical marker on your right notes the site of the town's first meetinghouse, built in 1700. Chatham's third and latest meetinghouse was moved in 1866 to its present site on Main Street and Old Harbor Road.

You may hear the drone of light planes from the nearby Chatham Airport, used primarily by private planes. Sight-seeing tours are available.

2.2 At intersection, veer left onto Old Queen Anne Road.

You are riding around the town forest.

2.6 At the stop sign, turn right onto Old Comers Road.

The Old Comers were the passengers who came to New England on board the *Mayflower*, the *Ann*, and the *Fortune*.

3.0 Turn left at a four-way stop onto Training Field Road.

3.7 Coast down to Route 28, the historic connecting road between Orleans and Chatham. Looking out for lines of traffic, especially in summer, cross to Fox Hill Road.

This road winds through Nickersons Neck, named after the town's first English settlers in what the Native Americans called Monomoit. William Nickerson bought much of the land here from the Native Americans and bought out the competing claims of the Old Comers' families.

During World War I, the neck was the site of a U.S. Naval Air Station that tested seaplanes and dirigibles in Chatham's frequent fogs. Its newsletter, the *Fly Paper*, circulated to the 13 officers and 145 enlisted men staffing the blimp hangar and seaplanes in 1920.

4.2 Turn left at bottom of hill.

Ride by Crow's Pond, an inlet of Pleasant Bay, a sheltered estuary behind the Nauset barrier beach. It leads to Bassing Harbor, sometimes a good place for catching striped bass.

Enjoy views of Eastward Ho! Golf Club, favorite links of the late House Speaker Tip O'Neill and Watergate lawyer James St. Clair.

4.9 Turn left onto Strong Island Road.

In 0.4 mile, from the town landing at the road's end, you have a great view across Pleasant Bay. To your right is Strong Island, preserved in perpetuity as conservation land. Look across to the barrier beach and its colony of beach camps.

Return the way you came along Strong Island Road.

5.7 Turn right onto Fox Hill Road.

6.4 Veer left onto Crow's Pond Road.

6.6 Turn left onto busy Route 28. Ride carefully.

Across Route 28 from Crow's Pond Road, behind a screen of trees, is the bowed roof of the 1664 Nickerson House, a reproduction that is home to the Nickerson family archives and to the genealogy of the thousands of Nickersons worldwide who can trace their lineage back to the family homestead nearby.

Ride past Ryders Cove, a popular harbor for pleasure craft, and the town-owned brick buildings, once home to the ship-to-shore radio transmitters for RCA (later MCI World-Com). The 30-acre complex, established in 1914, is listed on the National Register of Historic Places because of the building's unique brick construction. MCI sold the property at a bargain price in 1999. The town is still considering what to do with its new acquisition.

7.3 Turn right onto Crowell Road.

Enjoy a long, straight ride of nearly a mile. You'll pass the local high school on your right.

8.1 Turn left onto Stony Hill Road.

You'll be heading downhill with a bike path/sidewalk on your right, past a boatworks. Climb uphill to Route 28; you'll see the post office, restaurants, and a variety of stores, including a bike shop to your right.

8.5 Cross Route 28 on Stony Hill Road and into a neighborhood of summer cottages.

9.1 Turn right onto Old Harbor Road.

If you wish, you can coast straight for a quick look at the nearby harbor, the bay, and the North Beach camps, then ride back uphill and turn left onto Old Harbor Road.

Before the Revolution, Chatham had the Cape's largest maritime fleet, with 30 vessels and 240 men at sea.

10.7 At the stoplights on Route 28, turn left onto Shore Road.

You'll pass a mix of elegant homes, both old and new. Stop if you like at the Chatham Fish Pier to watch the commercial fishermen unload their catch. You can also catch a boat to North Beach or a tour to see and hear the harbor and gray seals that loll offshore.

You'll pass the prestigious Chatham Bars Inn, with a good pub, elegant dining, and a beach bar, all open to the public.

Author Joseph Lincoln spent summers along this road. Born in Brewster in 1870, he left the Cape at age 13 but made his name by writing more than 50 books based on the sea captains, village life, and Cape scenes that he remembered from his childhood.

11.8 Pass Main Street on your right, and in 0.25 mile turn left to the Chatham Lighthouse.

Now you're riding into the heart of Chatham, densely settled for most of its history. Stop to enjoy the view from Chatham Lighthouse, maintained by the U.S. Coast Guard. This area is known for its sandy beach below and its view of North Beach, with the waves breaking in the inlet to the Atlantic Ocean.

The first lighthouses here, built in 1808, were toppled by the

Susan Milton

From Chatham Light, you can see across the beach to the Atlantic.

sea's eroding waves by 1879. They were replaced by two new beacons at this site in 1877. One of the two towers was moved to
Eastham in 1923 to serve as Nauset Light.

12.3 *Back on Shore Road, dip to your right, then turn left onto
Morris Island Road.*

Morris Island Road is lined by summer houses and cottages at
sea level.

12.5 *The road turns right and crosses a causeway. To your right is
Stage Harbor.*

At the causeway's end, turn left onto Tisquantum Road and climb
a short hill.

13.4 *At Wikis Way, turn left to reach the Monomoy Wildlife Refuge
on Morris Island, open dawn to dusk. After visiting the refuge,
retrace your route, turning right off Wikis Way and then right
onto Morris Island Road to cross the causeway, with views of
boats and shellfishermen on your left, the salt marsh on your
right.*

The refuge here, with 40 acres and a 0.75-mile-long trail, is only a taste of the main event: the 2,750-acre refuge on Monomoy Island, accessible only by boat. The barrier-beach island, with sand dunes, freshwater ponds, and salt- and freshwater marshes, is haven to deer, seals, and other wildlife, but its main claim to fame is its migratory birds; Ludlow Griscom, a Chatham summer resident and dean of field ornithologists, estimates that the refuge is visited by more than 285 different species.

The domed weather observatory nearby is run by the U.S. Weather Service and is closed to the public.

14.5 *Turn left onto Bridge Street, which takes you to the Mitchell River Bridge. Cross the drawbridge, if the light is green.*

15.3 *Turn left onto Stage Harbor Road, which becomes Champlain Road.*

The road is named after the French explorer of these waters. Catch a glimpse of the Stage Harbor Lighthouse and the harbor beyond.

16.1 *Turn right onto Battlefield Road, then turn right onto Cedar Street.*

A bike path takes you past a mix of elegant and ordinary houses.

17.0 *Turn left onto Stage Harbor Road.*

17.3 *Coast to the Oyster Pond memorial and your tour's end, in sight of the spires and towers of the churches on Main Street in Chatham Center.*

Bicycle Repair Services

Bert and Carol's, 347 Orleans Rd., N. Chatham, MA 508-945-0137

Bikes and Blades, 195 Crowell Rd., Chatham, MA 508-945-7600

Dr. Gravity's Bike Shop, 564 Route 28, Harwichport, MA 508-430-0437

Harwichport Bike Co., 431 Route 28, Harwichport, MA 508-430-0200

Monomoy Sail & Cycle, 275 Orleans Rd., N. Chatham, MA 508-945-0811

Orleans Cycle, 26 Main St., Orleans, MA 508-255-9115

12

Brewster, Orleans, and Eastham

Distance: *23.4 miles*
Terrain: *Flat, with some rolling hills; mostly sheltered*

If you can imagine that Cape Cod stretches into the Atlantic Ocean like the arm of a posing muscleman, this trail leads along the inner elbow, where the three towns of Brewster, Orleans, and Eastham surround the tidal flats of Cape Cod Bay. At low tide you can walk for miles across the flats and through tidal pools. At high tide you can swim in the shallow, cool (but not frigid) water. This is a charming, easy tour through the marshes and the past that still link the three towns.

The Cape Cod Rail Trail here passes through quiet, shady woods, along salt marshes with views of the bay beyond, and through the hot, fertile upland of Eastham.

Eastham is proud of its history as the mother of several Lower Cape towns, including Orleans in 1797. Orleans developed into the business and social hub of the Lower Cape in the 1900s. Brewster, part of Harwich until 1803, grew quickly in the 1970s and 1980s to pass Orleans as the largest of the three towns.

Park at Nickerson State Park in Brewster, to the right of the main entrance. To reach the park from Route 6, take exit 12 and turn toward Brewster on Route 6A. The state park is well marked on your left, about 2 miles away. There's an alternate parking lot, west of the main entrance, near the seasonal Idle Times Bike Shop.

Tourist facilities are available at Salt Pond Visitors Center, Coast Guard Beach, Nauset Light Beach, Nickerson State Park, and Parish Park in Orleans Center.

0.0 *Start on the bike trail heading east from Nickerson State Park. The trail runs by the end of the parking lot. Turn right*

12 • Brewster, Orleans, and Eastham

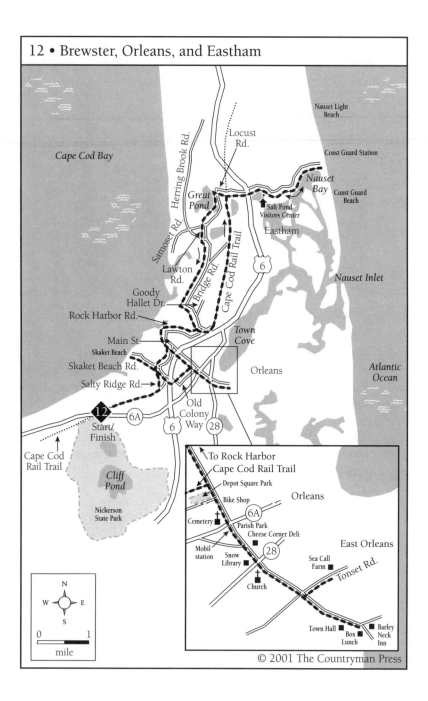

Cape Cod Bay

Nauset Light
Beach

Herring Brook Rd.

Locust
Rd.

Coast Guard Station

Great
Pond

Nauset
Bay

Coast Guard
Beach

Salt Pond
Visitors Center

Samoset Rd.

Eastham

Cape Cod Rail Trail

Lawton
Rd.

6

Bridge Rd.

Nauset Inlet

Goody
Hallet Dr.

Rock Harbor Rd.

Town
Cove

Main St.

Skaket Beach

Orleans

Atlantic
Ocean

Skaket Beach Rd.

Salty Ridge Rd.

12 6A

Old
Colony
Way

6 28

Start/
Finish

Cape Cod
Rail Trail

Cliff
Pond

Nickerson
State Park

To Rock Harbor
Cape Cod Rail Trail

Depot Square Park

Bike Shop

Orleans

Cemetery

6A

Parish Park

Cheese Corner Deli

East Orleans

Mobil
station

28

Snow
Library

Sea Call
Farm

Tonset Rd.

Church

N
W   E
S

0   1
mile

Town Hall Box
Lunch

Barley
Neck
Inn

© 2001 The Countryman Press

from the main lot (left from the alternate lot) and go through the tunnel under Route 6A.

This trail passes through the woods to the salt marsh that separates Orleans and Brewster. Look for lady's slippers along the trail in late May and June, goldenrod and purple asters in the fall.

1.8 *The trail detours onto Salty Ridge Road in Orleans. Climb the incline, bear left toward West Road, then turn right onto West Road toward Orleans Center. Cross over Route 6. At the base of the hill turn left onto the bike path, just before Old Colony Way.*

2.6 *Pass the Depot Square Park, built primarily for bicyclists, and turn right onto Main Street.*

Follow Main Street through Orleans Center, a scene that was painted by artist Edward Hopper. You'll pass a bike shop on your left. The Mobil station at the corner of Route 6A offers free air service. Diagonally across Route 6A are rest rooms behind Parish Park.

2.9 *Pass Snow Library on your right, then cross Route 28.*

Beyond Route 28 there are many Greek Revival houses that date back to the late 1800s. The Academy Playhouse, up a steep hill to your left, was the first Orleans Town Hall. The town hall then moved to the old elementary school, off Main Street to your right, across from the meetinghouse of the Orleans Historical Society. Soon a new town hall will be built, replacing the old school.

3.2 *Cross Tonset Road.*

4.2 *You'll come to the Barley Neck Inn.*

This inn was once the home of Captain Joseph D. Taylor, record-setting clipper-ship captain. Now the twice-restored 1857 building is an elegant restaurant and beach bar. This is the heart of the village of East Orleans. Kim's Café, Fancy's, and the Box Lunch are good places to grab a bite to eat and watch the beach traffic go by.

To find the waves of Nauset Beach, keep riding 1.4 miles along Main Street, which turns into Beach Road.

5.2 *Retrace your journey to Tonset Road. Turn right onto Tonset*

Road and go 0.3 mile to find Sea Call Farm, then retrace your route to Main Street.

This town-owned park was once a working farm overlooking Town Cove. Now it offers community gardens, picnicking, a haunted house in the fall, and a walk down to the shore.

5.8 *Turn right at Main Street and return to Depot Park.*

If you're still hungry, the Cheese Corner Deli on Main Street is well stocked with sandwiches, pastries, and excellent homemade Swedish breads.

6.4 *Continue past Depot Park on Main Street, which soon becomes Rock Harbor Road.*

To your right is the route for a bike path that will safely cross Route 6. The project is scheduled for completion in 2002. Until then, this narrow, busy road is the best route to reconnect with the Cape Cod Rail Trail. Fortunately, worried motorists and bicyclists seem to use extreme caution, and accidents are rare.

7.5 *At Rock Harbor, turn left to cycle around the harbor parking lot.*

At high tide in the summer, you can watch the sportfishing fleet unload bluefish, bass, and sometimes tuna. Sunset-watching is superb here. Overlooking the harbor is the Community of Jesus, known for its attractive gardens, concerts, Gregorian chants, and its large stone church.

This small harbor was a port for the packet boats that once ferried passengers and freight to Boston. The British tried to land here in 1814 to collect fees imposed on the many saltworks along the coast, but the invasion was repulsed by the town's militia after a brief skirmish.

When the railroad arrived, businesses around the harbor moved into Orleans Center.

8.5 *Leave the harbor parking lot, going straight along Rock Harbor Road. Ride along the winding road, passing Bridge Road and a county courthouse, to reach the entrance of the Cape Cod Rail Trail on your left.*

Follow the rail trail through salt marshes. To your left is the marsh

A wide path leads to the Nauset Coast Guard Station and its panoramic
view of the Atlantic Ocean and Nauset Bay.

around Rock Creek. To your right, across the highway, is Town Cove. The short distance between the creek and the cove has prompted several attempts to connect the two, first by way of Jeremiah's Gutter, named after Jeremiah Smith, an Eastham settler in the 1600s.

Now just a ditch, the waterway was big enough for small craft to squeeze through in the early 1700s. In 1804, Orleans and Eastham dug a small canal that was mainly used during the War of 1812 to barge salt away from a blockade of Cape Cod Bay.

11.2 *Turn right onto Locust Road, as directed by a brown sign pointing the way to the Cape Cod National Seashore. Coast downhill, then turn left onto Salt Pond Road. Using care, cross Route 6 at the stoplight. In 0.5 mile you'll reach the Salt Pond Visitors Center on your right. Watch for the bike path's abrupt end at the curb.*

The center's exhibits, films, and walking trails are a great introduction to the Cape, as well as to the National Seashore, established in 1961. About a third of Eastham lies within this national treasure.

11.7 *Pick up the bike trail to Coast Guard Beach, which starts at the yellow post.*

You meet walkers and other bicyclists along this trail, so be careful, especially on the many steep grades—which are surprisingly manageable.

13.3 *Emerge from the pine and oak woods to be rewarded by a view of extensive salt marsh backed by a barrier beach. Straight ahead is the bridge across the marsh to the picturesque Coast Guard station on the hill.*

13.6 *At the station, enjoy the view of the rolling combers on the beach below, or take a swim. Return the way you came, retracing your route to Locust Road.*

At the Coast Guard station, you can take in a stunning view of Nauset Marsh and the barrier beach, and you also have a chance to learn about how the power of the ocean changed the face of the Outer Beach. From the upper parking lot you can view Nauset

Inlet, which goes from the channel through the barrier beach on your left to the entrance of Salt Pond on your right.

16.0 *Pass by the rail trail and turn left onto Great Pond Road.*

Pause for a look at Great Pond, popular for swimming, fishing, and boating.

16.6 *At the stop sign turn right onto Samoset Road. Turn left onto Lawton Road.*

This part of town, known as the plains of Nauset, is blessed with rich, fertile soil where asparagus farms, turnip fields, and other truck gardens grew the produce that was shipped by train to Boston until the mid-1900s.

17.3 *Turn left onto Herring Brook Road and climb to the stop sign at Bridge Road, past the entrance to Herring Pond.*

18.3 *Turn right onto Bridge Road. Enjoy the ride, surrounded by a salt marsh. After the marsh, follow Bridge Road as it makes a 90-degree turn to your left (you could turn right on Bay View Road for a short detour overlooking the bay). Go past Goody Hallet Road on your right, site of a youth hostel, and enter Orleans.*

In the summer you'll see blue boxes in the marshes. They are traps for the fiercely biting greenhead fly.

19.9 *Turn right onto Rock Harbor Road and retrace your ride past Rock Harbor toward Orleans Center.*

21.2 *At the top of the hill, turn right onto Skaket Beach Road, paralleling Route 6. Veer right at the three-way intersection and end up at Skaket Beach, known for its sunset views and tidal flats.*

You pass the columns of the Captain Linnell House restaurant. In 1851, Captain Ebenezer Linnell modeled his home after a house he had seen near Marseilles, France, during his voyages as a clipper-ship captain.

21.6 *Back at the three-way intersection, veer right onto West Road. At the curve, make a sharp right onto Old West Road, which leads to the right onto Salty Ridge Road. You'll soon see the* *entrance to the Cape Cod Rail Trail; head west on this bike path toward Nickerson State Park.*

You pass a septic waste treatment plant on your left and Skaket Marsh, a natural treatment plant, on your right.

23.4 Finish at Nickerson State Park.

Bicycle Repair Services

Brewster Bike Shop, 442 Underpass Rd., Brewster, MA 508-896-8149

Idle Times Bike Shop, Route 6A, Brewster, MA 508-896-9242

Idle Times Bike Shop, Brackett Rd., N. Eastham, MA 508-255-8281

Little Capistrano Bike Shop, Route 6, Eastham, MA 508-255-6515

Orleans Cycle, 26 Main St., Orleans, MA 508-255-9115

Rail Trail Bikes & Blades, 302 Underpass Rd., Brewster, MA 508-896-8200

13
Around Eastham

Distance: 13.0 miles
Terrain: Flat, some inclines

"If you're fond of sand dunes, and salty air, quaint little villages here and there, you're sure to fall in love with Olde Cape Cod"—so croons Patti Page in a song that you may find yourself humming during this tour of sandy beaches on Cape Cod Bay and crashing waves along the dunes on the Atlantic Ocean.

This is the Cape Cod of long summer days, of perfect beach days that become golden memories. This tour will leave you with golden memories of the sound of sand crunching under your tires, the glint of blue water in Great Pond, the smell of pine trees and salt marshes, or the chill of a cool breeze off the water.

Such days and such summer memories lured many retirees and year-rounders here in the 1970s and 1980s, but off-season you'll still find isolated beaches, bone-chilling but invigorating winds, and a spare, essential landscape where the simple green of a cedar looks lush as you ride along these narrow bay roads.

This tour begins at the Salt Pond Visitors Center (phone: 508-255-3421) off Route 6 in Eastham. There are rest rooms, exhibits, water, and a telephone. Across the highway is a bike shop. Allow time to explore the center's trails and its exhibits about Cape Cod's history, the forces that shaped its shores, and the animals and plants that survive here.

Across Nauset Road the Old Schoolhouse Museum, bracketed by whale jawbones, chronicles Eastham's history as one of the largest Cape towns. It was incorporated as Eastham in 1641. Three Mayflower passengers were among the settlers who arrived here in 1646 to live among the Nauset tribe. The lands of Eastham stretched from what is now

13 • Around Eastham

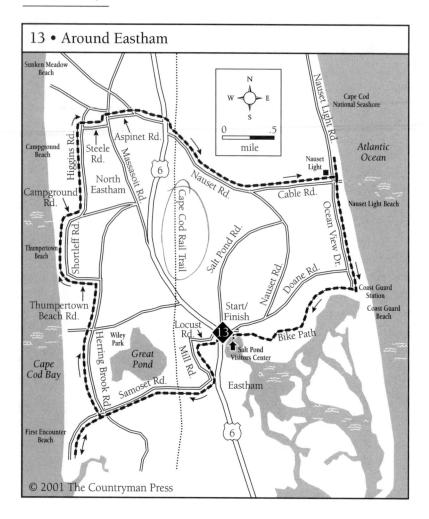

© 2001 The Countryman Press

Yarmouth to Truro. The museum is open 1–4 PM Monday through Friday in July and August; Saturday only in September.

0.0 *Turn left onto Nauset Road from the Salt Pond Visitors Center parking lot. Cross Route 6 at the stoplight. Turn right onto Locust Road at the stop sign.*

Many houses here date from the mid-1800s or earlier. To your right is a half-Cape, built in 1765. On your left is a full Cape, built in 1795. Across Locust Road is a beautiful Greek Revival house, built in 1850.

0.3 *Turn left onto Mill Road, then turn right at the mill onto Depot Road, which feeds into Samoset Road.*

This leads to a magnificent side view of Eastham's windmill, moved to this site in 1808 after perhaps a century of service. According to local legend, millwright Thomas Paine of Eastham probably built the mill in the late 1600s in Plymouth. The smock-style mill was moved to Truro in the 1770s and, in 1793, to the shores of Eastham's salt pond. The mill is open 10–5 Monday through Saturday, and 1–5 Sundays in July and August. The windmill green is still a gathering place for town celebrations and festivals.

1.1 *To your right is the Chapel in the Pines, a Unitarian church and, on Saturday nights, a coffeehouse with folksingers.*

To your left, go by the Cape Cod Rail Trail. Pass Great Pond Road on your right and Jemima Pond on your left, then stop at the four-way stop at Herring Brook Road.

2.0 *Cross Herring Brook Road. Ride along the salt marsh to First Encounter Beach, where in 1620 Pilgrims from the Mayflower and Native Americans encountered each other for the first time, exchanging arrows and musket balls. Then retrace your route on Samoset Road.*

3.6 *Turn left onto Herring Brook Road.*

You pass Wiley Park, town-owned conservation land on Great Pond, with bathrooms open summer until Labor Day.

A series of roads to your left leads to small bay beaches—Thumpertown, Campground, and South Sunken Meadow—to sample at will.

Names such as "Thumpertown" and "Campground" recall the days of summer Methodist camps—in the early 1800s—later replaced by summer and year-round homes and rentals.

4.9 *Turn left onto Thumpertown Beach Road, then right onto Shurtleff Road. Watch out for sand in the road.*

The bay road is lined with houses that block any view of the bay, although they do create a picturesque windbreak.

The old Eastham windmill, a local landmark.

5.8 At Campground Beach, veer right onto Campground Road. At the stop sign, turn right.

This is a classic Cape summer neighborhood, where kids can walk by themselves to the beach or play in the road.

6.3 Turn left onto Higgins Road.

7.0 Turn right onto Steele Road.

7.3 Turn left onto Massasoit Road, and then quickly turn right

onto Aspinet Road, which leads you to Route 6.

If you were to remain on Massasoit Road, the nature trails and exhibits of the Wellfleet Bay Wildlife Sanctuary of the Massachusetts Audubon Society would be a mile straight ahead—after the Wellfleet Drive-In and its flea markets.

7.9 *At Route 6, turn right. Take care to stay on the sidewalk until you reach the stoplight at Nauset Road. Cross the highway to follow Nauset Road.*

You'll soon pass the entrance to the Cape Cod Rail Trail.

8.9 *Turn left onto Cable Road.*

There's no street sign here, only a brown national park sign pointing to the high school and Nauset Light Beach. Pass the Nauset Regional High School on your left.

9.6 *Look for the white posts and a FIRE ROAD sign on your left.*

This is the only marker for the Three Sisters lighthouses, moved back from the ocean to this grassy oasis. These wooden towers were built in 1892; in 1923, they were replaced by the Nauset Light. From the Three Sisters, a paved trail leads to Nauset Light Beach, crowned by the flashing red beacon to your left.

For a short detour, cycle down the road to your left to see where hungry winter storms have gnawed away the road. In 1997, townspeople and lighthouse fans raced to move the lighthouse to a safe site, off the eroding cliffs.

10.2 *Back at the beach entrance, coast down Ocean View Drive heading south.*

The road lives up to its name after the first half mile. Compare this scenic area to the bay shore, which is unprotected by the National Seashore restrictions.

11.0 *The woods open onto a magnificent panorama of surf, beach, and the Coast Guard Station. Coast downhill and bicycle up to the station.*

The station was built in 1936 to replace the original, built in 1915, which was threatened by rapidly eroding shores. The second station was taken out of service in 1958. Now National Seashore personnel stay here.

Coast Guard Beach has outdoor showers, a bathhouse, and exhibits that are worth a stop. Take a swim, a beach walk, or a rest here.

The upper lot overlooks the Nauset estuary, shared with Orleans. You can also see the former site of a bathhouse and parking lot that were destroyed by the waves of the Great Blizzard of 1978. Also destroyed was the Outermost House, the beach cottage where naturalist Henry Beston lived in 1927–28, a year he chronicled in his book of the same name.

11.8 *From the rotary, where the shuttle bus stops in season, take the bike trail back to the Salt Pond Visitors Center. Follow the trail downhill, testing your brakes. Cross the salt marsh that curves around to the entrance to Salt Pond.*

Bicyclists and walkers share the trail, which requires cooperation and cordiality.

13.0 *Reach the Salt Pond Visitors Center and the end of the tour.*

There are two good walking trails to explore from the visitors center: the Nauset Marsh Trail, which skirts Salt Pond, its salt marsh, and woods; and the Buttonbush Trail, built so that blind visitors could hear, smell, and feel the Cape's natural beauty.

Bicycle Repair Services

Black Duck Bike Shop, LeCount Hollow Rd., S. Wellfleet, MA 508-349-9801

Idle Times Bike Shop, Brackett Rd., N. Eastham, MA 508-255-8281

Little Capistrano Bike Shop, Route 6, Eastham, MA 508-255-6515

Orleans Cycle, 26 Main St., Orleans, MA 508-255-9115

Wellfleet Cycles, 54 E. Commercial Street, Wellfleet, MA 508-349-9322

14
North Eastham and South Wellfleet

Distance: *21.0 miles*
Terrain: *Long inclines; exposed riding conditions*

Everywhere you go on Cape Cod, you are reminded of the cycles of life, whether in nature or in the affairs of the people who live on these shores.

Look at Nauset Light, for example, in its historic and picturesque setting overlooking the Atlantic Ocean at the start of this tour. This light once was one of Chatham's Twin Sisters, well-known beacons to mariners. In the early 1920s, it was separated from its twin and moved to this station. In 1997, when it was less than 50 feet from the eroding edge, the light was moved again, this time across the road, inch by inch, to its present site. The Nauset Lighthouse Preservation Society raised more than $250,000 to move the steel and brick structure intact.

Long a maritime guide, Nauset Light is now a beacon for consumers. The Nauset Light is prominently displayed on all bags of Cape Cod Potato Chips, a Cape-hatched product. The beacon is also on the Barnstable County lighthouse license plate.

Start this tour at Nauset Light Beach in Eastham. The beach, part of the National Seashore, offers bathrooms, water, a telephone, bike racks, and a great view of the Atlantic Ocean. With the ocean at your back, take the paved trail out of the parking lot.

0.0 Go straight onto Cable Road.

This road was named for the telegraph cable that connected Brest, France, and Eastham, near Nauset Light, in 1879. In 1898 the undersea cable was moved to enter Town Cove at Orleans, where the former cable station is now the French Cable Station Museum.

0.7 Pass Nauset Regional High School on your right. Take an immediate right onto Nauset Road.

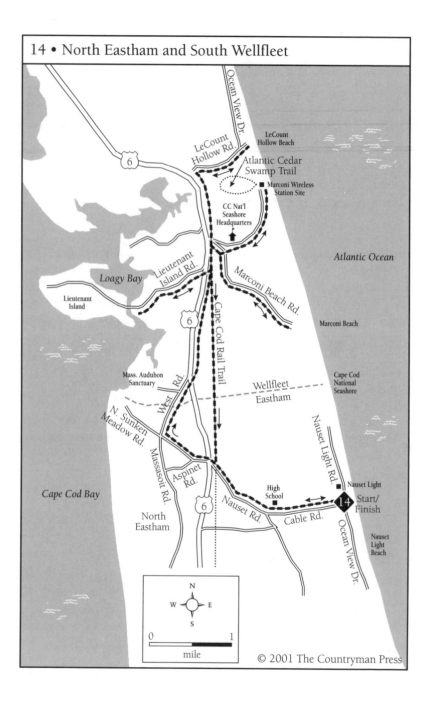

Ocean View Dr.

LeCount Hollow Rd.

LeCount Hollow Beach

Atlantic Cedar Swamp Trail

■ Marconi Wireless Station Site

CC Nat'l Seashore Headquarters

Atlantic Ocean

Lieutenant Island Rd.

Loagy Bay

Marconi Beach Rd.

Lieutenant Island

6

Marconi Beach

Cape Cod Rail Trail

Mass. Audubon Sanctuary

West Rd.

Wellfleet
Eastham

Cape Cod National Seashore

N. Sunken Meadow Rd.

Massasoit Rd.

Aspinet Rd.

Nauset Light Rd.

High School ■

Nauset Light ■

6

Nauset Rd.

Cable Rd.

14 Start/ Finish

North Eastham

Cape Cod Bay

Ocean View Dr.

Nauset Light Beach

N
W ⊕ E
S

0 — 1
mile

© 2001 The Countryman Press

This high school can be an alternate starting site in season, when the National Seashore is charging a fee for parking. This school serves students from Eastham, Wellfleet, Orleans, and Brewster.

1.7 *Cross Route 6 at the stoplight. Turn right onto the paved sidewalk, then turn left onto Aspinet Road.*

1.9 *Veer right onto North Sunken Meadow Road.*

Much of the land to the right was bought by Eastham for a public drinking water supply and other municipal uses still under discussion.

2.4 *Turn right onto Massasoit Road, marked only by a stop sign. This road's name changes to West Road as you enter Wellfleet.*

As you ride up and down the road's hills, you'll pass a trailer park and one of the last drive-in theaters in the United States. On weekends the drive-in hosts a flea market where vendors sell antique postcards, irregular socks, honesty (a plant), and many other treasures to tourists and locals.

3.2 *Turn left from West Road into the Wellfleet Bay Wildlife Sanctuary, managed by the Massachusetts Audubon Society.*

The earth-friendly building, gardens, and exhibits of the sanctuary are 0.3 mile away and worth a visit. The sanctuary covers 1,000 acres of pine woods, moors, and salt marshes, where you may see egrets, painted turtles, cedar waxwings, whimbrels, great horned owls, and many other Cape natives and visitors. Call 508-349-2615 for a daily schedule of programs.

3.8 *Back at West Road, turn left to approach Route 6. Turn left onto Route 6 (the shoulder is wide here).*

5.1 *Turn left onto Lieutenant Island Road.*

This road leads to a marshy headland on Loagy Bay. Lieutenant Island is likely named for Lieutenant Anthony, a Native American who lived in Wellfleet in the 1600s. Former president Grover Cleveland came here to hunt ducks when the island was known as Horse Island.

6.0 *Stop at the bridge that crosses Loagy Bay and check the tide. Retrace your route to Route 6.*

The eroded cliffs and wide beach near Nauset Light

At high tide, island residents are cut off from the mainland and must park on either side of this bridge, waiting for a chance to splash across.

7.1 At Route 6, cross into the parking lot of Rookie's restaurant (stop for a pizza, if you like). Take the bluestone path to the Cape Cod Rail Trail, then turn left onto the bike path.

7.5 Turn right into the Cape Cod National Seashore. Go straight to reach Marconi Beach.

This is a lovely, long bike ride through pine woods to the ocean.

8.9 Arrive at Marconi Beach, where there are rest rooms, open seasonally.

Enjoy access to the beach, stretching for miles in either direction, before retracing your route back to the road intersection.

10.4 At the intersection, before you reach Route 6, turn right and travel past the national seashore headquarters.

This was the former site of Camp Wellfleet, a National Guard training camp, abandoned in 1961. Antiaircraft guns would practice on gliders in the wind currents created by the bluffs here. This spot has been rediscovered by hang-gliding enthusiasts.

11.4 Arrive at the Marconi Wireless Station site and Atlantic Cedar Swamp Trail. After visiting, leave the parking lot and return to the road intersection, just after the park headquarters.

On January 18, 1903, the first two-way transatlantic wireless message was sent from this site between President Theodore Roosevelt and King Edward II of England. A display chronicles inventor Guglielmo Marconi's work here and in Nova Scotia.

The Atlantic Cedar Swamp Trail, just off the Marconi Station parking lot, wanders through pine woods; the trees increase in size as you move inland. The 1.2-mile trail ends at a cedar swamp in a kettle hole.

12.4 Turn right at the road intersection. Just before the stoplight at Route 6, turn right onto the Cape Cod Rail Trail.

12.7 Pass the Old North Cemetery and its interesting gravestones.

13.2 The rail trail takes you into LeCount Hollow parking lot. Turn right onto LeCount Hollow Road.

Upon reaching South Wellfleet, you'll find an information booth, a post office, a fried-clam and sub shop, and a small convenience store, as well as a bicycle shop.

13.8 At Ocean View Drive, cross the road to LeCount Hollow Beach. After enjoying the beach, retrace your journey to the Lecount Hollow parking lot of the Cape Cod Rail Trail.

This beach is popular with surfers because of its long waves.

15.0 Turn left back onto the rail trail.

Many restaurants and businesses along this stretch of the bike trail, which was completed in 1995, have put out the welcome rack for bicyclists. Rookies, the Sub'N'Cone, and Poit's all have fans of their pizza, sandwiches, and fried clams.

19.1 An asphalt plant's mixing towers (and sometimes noise and dust) greet you at Nauset Road, where you turn left.

20.0 Turn left onto Cable Road and pass the high school.

21.0 End the tour at Nauset Light Beach, where you began.

Bicycle Repair Services

Black Duck Bike Shop, LeCount Hollow Rd., S. Wellfleet, MA 508-349-9801

Galeforce Bike Rentals, 144 Bradford St. Ext., Provincetown, MA 508-487-4849

Idle Times Bike Shop, Brackett Rd., N. Eastham, MA 508-255-8281

Little Capistrano Bike Shop, Route 6, Eastham, MA 508-255-6515

Nelson's Bike Shop, 43 Race Point Rd., Provincetown, MA 508-487-8849

Orleans Cycle, 26 Main St., Orleans, MA 508-255-9115

Wellfleet Cycles, 54 E. Commercial Street, Wellfleet, MA 508-349-9322

15
Around Wellfleet

Distance: *23.5 miles*
Terrain: *Hilly, some long inclines; exposed riding conditions*

In 1894, the motto of the Wellfleet graduating class was "Row, don't drift," records historian Judy Stetson in her book, *Wellfleet: A Pictorial History*. Wellfleeters knew firsthand how to get places in life, whether from a ship in the harbor or to an exotic port elsewhere in the world.

Wellfleet native Lorenzo Dow Baker had left the Cape as a ship's captain and returned home a successful tycoon and founder of what became the United Fruit Company. In 1870, he picked up a cargo of bananas in Jamaica for 25 cents a bunch to fill his returning ship. He sold the overripe novelty in Boston for $3 a bunch. He learned to buy the fruit green and pioneered the banana trade. When he summered here before his death in 1906, a bunch of bananas was always hanging on his porch, free for the picking. Isaac Rich, born here in 1801, was a fish dealer who ultimately helped found Boston University and left the institution nearly $1 million in his will. They were just two among many sea captains, sailors, and merchants in trade and shipping out of Wellfleet Harbor in the 1800s.

Wellfleet, once known as Billingsgate, was made separate from Eastham in 1763, and it quickly started rowing. Only 8 miles long and 3 miles wide, the town's assets were ocean and bay beaches, freshwater ponds, good soil for farming, and good bottom for shellfishing. What more could anyone ask? Visitors agreed, and the summer trade began in the early 20th century. After World War II, visitors were no longer a novelty but a part of summer life.

Blessed with a town center and a strong identity, Wellfleet has built a reputation as an arts center because of its fine galleries and provocative

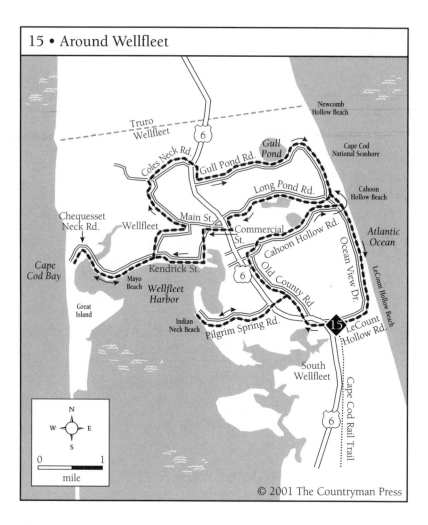

© 2001 The Countryman Press

theater. For bicyclists, whose motto could be "Pedal, don't coast," the town is blessed by the Cape Cod Rail Trail, a variety of scenery, and quiet roads.

This tour starts in the parking lot at the end of the Cape Cod Rail Trail, off LeCount Hollow Road. From the Mid-Cape, take Route 6 into Wellfleet to LeCount Hollow Road and turn right. The parking lot is 0.1 mile on your right.

0.0 Turn left onto LeCount Hollow Road.

The LeCount family lived in the hollow at the end of this road as late as 1872.

0.1 *Turn right onto Route 6.*

0.4 *Turn right onto Old County Road, just before a gas station.*

This former part of the King's Highway to Provincetown is a quiet, little-traveled road through Cape woods.

0.9 *Turn left onto Spring Valley Road, at the base of a small hill.*

1.3 *Cross Route 6, then jog left to enter Pilgrim Spring Road.*

2.0 *At the stop sign, veer left.*

3.0 *You arrive at Indian Neck Beach. Watch out for sand in the road.*

This was a popular camping spot for Native Americans, judging from the wealth of arrowheads, stone tools, and other relics once found here.

Enjoy a panoramic view of your day's travels. To your right is Wellfleet Harbor with its fleet of fishing boats and pleasure craft. Straight ahead are the church towers in Wellfleet Center. To your left are Chequesset Neck and Great Island.

In 1849, shipbuilder Edward Rogers was still a boy, and he marveled at the sight of the sailing fleet of 80 or more vessels in Wellfleet Harbor. "They could not have been worth less than $200,000 and they were owned by their crews, numbering about a thousand men."

5.1 *Retrace your route back to Old County Road, crossing Route 6 with caution. Turn left onto Old County Road.*

6.3 *Turn right at the road's end onto Cahoon Hollow Road, which is unmarked. A rail fence is across from the intersection.*

The road leads past Great Pond, a deep kettle pond. The kettle, a steep-sided hole, is created when a glacial remnant melts away. If the hole is deep enough to reach the water table, the kettle fills.

7.7 *At Ocean View Drive, cross for the promised ocean view.*

Continue straight to Cahoon Hollow Beach, down a hill to the Beachcomber restaurant and bar, a summer club popular with surfers and music fans.

8.0 *Backtrack to Ocean View Drive, turn right and then left onto Long Pond Road.*

9.3 *Pass Long Pond on your left.*

Or stop for a dip in the cool waters of this kettle pond.

10.0 *Cross Route 6 on a highway bridge. Slow down immediately to stop at Main Street. Turn right onto Main Street, which has a sidewalk, and climb a short hill into Wellfleet Center.*

Enjoy the skyline created by the steeples of the United Methodist Church and of the Wellfleet Congregational Church, which rings ship's time. On a ship, there are six watches, four hours each, per day. Bells mark each half hour. For the watch that begins at noon, one bell rings at 12:30 PM; eight bells ring at 4 PM.

The churches and elegant homes are a visible sign of Wellfleet's wealth during the late 1800s.

10.3 *Turn left onto Bank Street. There's a crosswalk in front of the Wellfleet Town Hall.*

On Bank Street you'll pass the Blue Heron Gallery, one of many fine galleries ahead.

10.4 *Veer right onto Commercial Street, at the bottom of the hill.*

For a short side trip, turn left to see Uncle Tim's Bridge, a wooden walkway across Duck Creek and its marshes. Once the water was deep enough here that schooners could tie up to this bridge. But a railroad bridge sealed off the harbor to all but boats small enough to pass under.

Until the early 1900s, there were 30 acres of shellfish flats and oyster shacks along Duck Creek. Boats would beach just off Commercial Street. Still a street of business, Commercial Street is now lined with art galleries—Cove, Left Bank, Sandpiper, and Brehmer Graphics—and restaurants.

11.0 *Commercial Street becomes Kendrick after the road veers sharply right around the harbor.*

Wellfleet Harbor is a place where people gather for coffee, sun, fishing, boating, bicycling, and work. The Bookstore Restaurant and Capt. Higgins' Seafood offer Wellfleet oysters and other shellfish, a delicacy for decades. The Wellfleet Harbor Actors' Theater (WHAT) stages intriguing original plays.

A mooring in one of the Cape's many kettle ponds

Susan Milton

11.7 Go past Mayo Beach and veer left uphill onto Chequesset Neck Road.

Enjoy the views of the harbor on your left. Pass by the Chequesset Neck Yacht and Country Club on your right.

13.0 Cross the Herring River dike to Great Island.

There's a landing on your left, across the bridge, which is a popular resting place.

13.4 Turn left into the parking lot for Great Island.

This National Seashore attraction is the start of a beautiful 8-mile hike along the shores of this barrier beach, once an island and now a peninsula.

In the early 1700s, fishermen climbed lookout towers here to watch for whales, which they'd try to trap along these shores. Now people try to save the whales that beach here.

There's no fresh water here, and only portable toilets. The high ridge is Sunset Hill, a popular evening destination that overlooks Cape Cod Bay.

15.1 Retrace your route on Chequesset Neck Road and, at the intersection with Kendrick Street, veer left toward Wellfleet Center.

15.8 Turn left onto Holbrook Road at the stop sign, then turn left immediately onto West Main Street and pass the town library in a former candle factory.

Or turn right into Wellfleet Center. The town hall is at the opposite end of Main Street. There are many art galleries, beautiful old buildings, shops, and a few restaurants that can easily occupy an hour or two.

16.1 Veer right at the fork and pass High Toss Road.

17.0 Turn right onto Coles Neck Road, near the Truro border.

17.7 Turn right at the stop sign. Carefully approach Route 6 and its speeding cars. Turn right onto the highway and travel 0.3 mile to its intersection with Gull Pond Road.

18.1 Turn left onto Gull Pond Road, which is also the road to New-comb Hollow Beach.

Winding and bumpy, this is a great example of an old Cape Cod road. It's scenic, but worrisome when cars and bicycles must share.

19.1 *Pass the town landing at Gull Pond, another chance to sample a Cape kettle hole pond.*

A few feet away is the Samuel Rider House. Built in the late 1700s, the building preserves the ambience of a Cape farmhouse and its outbuildings.

19.4 *At the stop sign, veer left onto Gross Hill Road. Start climbing to the cliffs along the ocean.*

20.1 *Turn right onto Ocean View Drive. Travel through dunes covered with dense thickets; here and there, gaps in the thickets offer views.*

To your left is Newcomb Hollow Beach, half a mile away.

22.8 *Turn right onto LeCount Hollow Road.*

23.5 *On your left is the parking lot for the Cape Cod Rail Trail, where your tour began.*

Bicycle Repair Services

Black Duck Bike Shop, LeCount Hollow Rd., S. Wellfleet, MA 508-349-9801

Galeforce Bike Rentals, 144 Bradford St. Ext., Provincetown, MA 508-487-4849

Idle Times Bike Shop, Brackett Rd., N. Eastham, MA 508-255-8281

Little Capistrano Bike Shop, Route 6, Eastham, MA 508-255-6515

Nelson's Bike Shop, 43 Race Point Rd., Provincetown, MA 508-487-8849

Wellfleet Cycles, 54 E. Commercial Street, Wellfleet, MA 508-349-9322

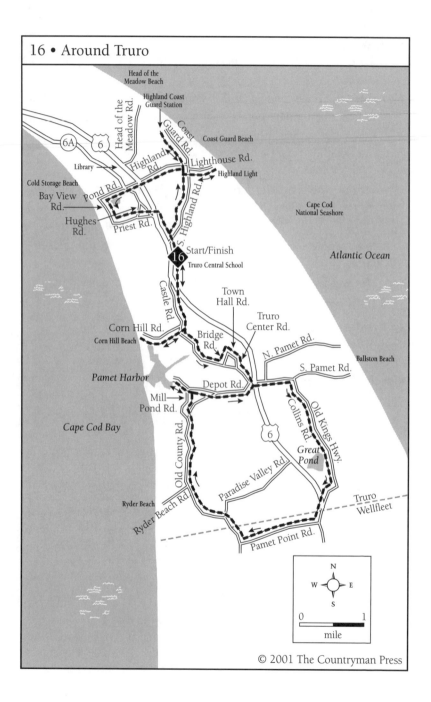

Head of the
Meadow Beach

Highland Coast
Guard Station

Head of the Meadow Rd.

Coast Guard Rd.

Coast Guard Beach

6A

6

Library

Highland Rd.

Lighthouse Rd.

Highland Light

Cold Storage Beach

Pond Rd.

S. Highland Rd.

Cape Cod
National Seashore

Bay View
Rd.

Hughes
Rd.

Priest Rd.

Atlantic Ocean

16 Start/Finish

Truro Central School

Castle Rd.

Town
Hall Rd.

Truro
Center Rd.

Corn Hill Rd.

Bridge
Rd.

Corn Hill Beach

N. Pamet Rd.

S. Pamet Rd.

Ballston Beach

Pamet Harbor

Depot Rd.

Mill
Pond Rd.

Cape Cod Bay

Old County Rd.

6

Collins Rd.

Old Kings Hwy.

Great
Pond

Ryder Beach

Ryder Beach Rd.

Paradise Valley Rd.

Truro
Wellfleet

Pamet Point Rd.

N
W E
S

0   1
mile

© 2001 The Countryman Press

16
Around Truro

Distance: *22.7 miles*
Terrain: *Hilly and demanding, but rewarding*

Many people just drive through Truro on their way to Provincetown. Their loss, our gain. Long bypassed in the 20th century, Truro has preserved the charm of its winding roads, quiet pine and oak woods, river valleys, moors, and sea cliffs.

At the end of the 17th century, the Pamet tribe sold land here to English settlers in Eastham. The town incorporated in 1709, taking the name of Cornwall's counterpart, Truro, which means "place of the hill" in Cornish. Make that "hills": A series of deep valleys cuts across the high plains of Truro. Geologists argue whether they were cut by streams from melting glaciers or eroded by streams escaping from a lake. Either way, they create a constantly changing scene.

A thriving whaling and fishing port through the 1800s, for years Truro was too remote and rural to attract much investment. Now the many new houses, a new school, a new library and a new police and fire station all reflect the town's growth and change.

Notice the difference between the "back side" of Truro in the Cape Cod National Seashore and the bay side of Truro, largely unprotected from development.

Edward Hopper lived here and painted the golden light that bathes Truro landscapes. Photographer Joel Meyerowitz captures the same light decades later. Writers Edmund Wilson, Edna St. Vincent Millay, and Annie Dillard have all enjoyed Truro beaches and woods.

As Judith Rossner depicted in her novel *August*, Truro beaches have long attracted therapists seeking sanity in summer. There's really no need to analyze the town's charm. Just enjoy.

This tour begins at the Truro Central School, on the southeast side of Route 6.

0.0 Turn right onto Route 6 and climb uphill.

0.3 Turn right onto South Highland Road.

Follow signs to Highland Light (officially Cape Cod Light). This was the site of the Cape's first lighthouse, built overlooking the "Graveyard of the Atlantic," the dangerous stretch between Monomoy Island and Race Point.

1.6 Turn right onto Lighthouse Road.

To your left is the Truro Historical Museum, hidden each spring by a bank of wisteria. The museum is open 10–5 daily from June until mid-September to display its fishing and whaling gear, ship-wreck mementos, ship's models, furnishings, and works of art.

The museum is in the old Highland House guest house, which opened in 1862 and was home to 100 guests at a time. Beyond the museum is the Highland Light Golf Course, built in 1892.

Straight ahead is Highland Light, the second beacon built on this spot since 1797. Naturalist and author Henry David Thoreau stayed here in the keeper's house for 3 days during one of his long beach walks in the mid-1800s. The cliffs erode about 3 feet a year, a visible reminder of the sea's power. By 1926, only 4 acres remained of the original 10-acre site purchased in 1796. In 1996, prodded by local residents, the government moved the lighthouse 450 feet to the safety of the golf course's seventh hole.

To your right, glimpse an odd twosome: the Jenny Lind Tower—moved here in 1927—a memorial to the Swedish sopra-no who sang from the granite tower in the mid-1800s when it was part of the Fitchburg railroad depot; and the "golf ball" radar dome run by the Federal Aviation Administration. This site tracks all air activity from Bangor, Maine, south to New York City and from Albany, New York, east 200 miles out over the Atlantic.

1.7 After retracing your route, turn right onto South Highland Road.

The road becomes Coast Guard Road, exposed to sun and wind.

2.5 At the Highland Coast Guard station, there's access to the beach below for a walk along the crashing waves.

Susan Milton

Summer cottages near a secluded Truro bay beach

3.3 *Reversing course on Coast Guard Road, turn right onto Highland Road. This leads under Route 6 to a flashing red light at Shore Road (Route 6A).*

At the intersection is Dutra's Market, a good place to stock up for a hot, thirsty ride through Truro's Pond Village. The junction also is the terminus for a summer shuttle for passengers and bicycles between Truro and Provincetown. Across Shore Road, on your right, is the town's former grammar school, later an art gallery, offices, and fishnet factory. Pond Village also was the site of the Cape's first cold-storage plant, which allowed fresh fish to be shipped inland.

4.3 *Cross Shore Road (Route 6A) to Pond Road.*

This road leads to Cape Cod Bay past Pilgrim Pond. Sixteen Pilgrims camped here in 1620 on their second night in the New World. How could they ever leave this spot?

4.8 *Pedal uphill for a gorgeous view of the bay, just steps from secluded Cold Storage Beach.*

The Provincetown Pilgrim Monument stands to your right. To

your left, the bay shore curves in to Wellfleet. Look back and see Highland Light, flashing over the pond. You're standing on an embankment built for the railroad in the 1870s.

4.9 *Heading back, at the foot of the hill, turn sharply right onto Bay View Road, previously called Railroad Avenue.*

You'll climb onto an exposed moor, once empty and now dotted with houses and cottages.

5.4 *Turn left onto Priest Road. At the fork, veer left onto Hughes Road, then turn right onto Route 6A and climb uphill.*

To your left is the Truro Vineyards, with tastings weekly.

6.1 *Turn right onto Route 6. Ride carefully here.*

You'll pass the elementary school, police and fire station, a liquor store, and other shops as you watch for Castle Road.

7.2 *Turn right onto Castle Road.*

This is the scenic route to Corn Hill. Here the Pilgrims landed in 1620 and plundered the Native Americans' supplies of corn. Small wonder the next Native Americans they encountered shot arrows at them at First Encounter Beach in Eastham.

7.9 *Turn right onto Corn Hill Road.*

This road travels through one of Truro's many picturesque valleys.

8.5 *Arrive at Corn Hill Beach, where the bay is deep and cool.*

There are no conveniences here except portable toilets and two soda machines, but the sight of Corn Hill itself is worth the stop.

9.0 *Back at Castle Road, turn right as the road cuts along a hillside overlooking salt marshes.*

9.7 *Pass the Castle Hill Center for the Arts at the intersection with Meetinghouse Road.*

This is an Outer Cape center for the arts, from pottery-making to lectures by well-known writers and artists.

10.3 *Veer right in front of the original library's concrete wall and pass by a grocery store.*

The town green to the left is a favorite place for anything from early morning tai chi to croquet on weekends.

10.4 *Turn left to pass under Route 6 to the Pamet Roads. Pass by the end of North Pamet Road to your left.*

In November 1991, storm-pushed waves overwashed Pamet Road, cutting the road into two parts that end at Ballston Beach. At the end of North Pamet Road is the former youth hostel, a working cranberry bog under restoration by the Cape Cod National Seashore, and, up the nearby hill, a magnificent view. Then-vice-president Al Gore and his family enjoyed that view on a 1996 summer vacation. But the road itself is very narrow, with little room for a car and a bicycle.

10.4 *Turn right, for a safer ride along South Pamet Road.*

The intersection of the Pamet Roads is a favorite launching place for canoeists.

11.0 *Veer right at the intersection with Collins Road.*

You're now on part of the former King's Highway, traveling uphill through the tall pines.

For a nice side trip, go straight 1 mile to Ballston Beach.

Little is left of the resort created here in 1891 by S. Osborne Ball. Five generations summered here, enjoying the beach, the dining hall, the bowling alley, and the ballroom of Ballston Heights. Only a cottage or two remains, half buried in the sand.

Retrace your route to Collins Road and turn left.

12.5 *After a glimpse of Great Pond, the road takes a sharp right, off the old highway.*

13.2 *At the bottom of a hill, turn left and arrive at Route 6. Turn left onto Route 6 and you'll soon enter the town of Wellfleet.*

13.7 *Turn right onto Pamet Point Road. Wind downhill through woods to the bay.*

14.9 *Turn right onto Old County Road.*

This part of the tour overlooks Prince Valley. Be careful, as you'll most likely want to gaze at the scenery.

16.2 *Pass Ryder Beach Road on Old County Road.*

For a 1.2-mile-long side trip, turn left onto Ryder Beach Road. At the corner on your left is a parcel of preserved land that is awash with colors of highbush blueberries and swamp maples in autumn. At the beach, walk across the dunes to the shore.

17.4 *Turn left onto Mill Pond Road, heading toward Pamet Harbor and past 200-year-old farmhouses.*

At one time, this was a bustling part of Truro that sent 60 Pamet schooners to pursue the spring and fall mackerel migrations. But in the 1850s the harbor started silting in, and people moved away. The population dropped from 2,050 in 1850 to 972 by 1900. In the 1920s, the town dug a new channel into the harbor; now it's alive with pleasure boats.

17.9 *At the fork, turn left onto Depot Road and arrive at scenic Pamet Harbor, filled like an overflowing bowl at high tide. On your return, veer left to stay on Depot Road.*

18.3 *Turn left onto Old County Road.*

18.8 *Turn left onto Castle Road.*

You can stay on Castle Road to Route 6 or take a side trip through Truro history via its town hall and graveyard.

20.0 *Veer right onto Truro Center Road in front of the old library and pedal or walk uphill.*

20.4 *Turn left onto Town Hall Road and climb another hill.*

At the top of the hill, find the First Congregational Church on your left; its 18th-century graveyard is full of poignant epitaphs about Truro's past residents.

20.5 *Turn left again onto Bridge Road and head downhill to Castle Road.*

20.8 *Turn right onto Castle Road, which winds around past Corn Hill Road and climbs up a long hill to Route 6.*

22.3 *At Route 6, turn left. Stay on the shoulder of the highway and pedal uphill.*

22.7 *Arrive at the Truro Central School, where this tour began.*

Bicycle Repair Services

Black Duck Bike Shop, LeCount Hollow Rd., S. Wellfleet, MA 508-349-9801

Galeforce Bike Rentals, 144 Bradford St. Ext., Provincetown, MA 508-487-4849

Idle Times Bike Shop, Brackett Rd., N. Eastham, MA 508-255-8281

Little Capistrano Bike Shop, Route 6, Eastham, MA 508-255-6515

Nelson's Bike Shop, 43 Race Point Rd., Provincetown, MA 508-487-8849

Wellfleet Cycles, 54 E. Commercial Street, Wellfleet, MA 508-349-9322

17
Provincetown and North Truro

Distance: *20.2 miles*
Terrain: *Hilly on trails, flat on roads; exposed to weather*

The Pilgrims landed here in 1620, on their way to Plymouth. Pilgrims are still coming here in search of whales to watch, fresh fish, food, freedom to live as they wish, and the beauty of a well-preserved shore town and summer resort.

This is where Eugene O'Neill got his start as a playwright in 1916. Journalist Mary Heaton Vorse, writer John Dos Passos, and U.S. poet laureate Stanley Kunitz are just a few of the writers who have summered or lived in Provincetown.

In Provincetown, anything is possible. You will find classic Colonial houses with figureheads from whaling ships and tacky beach cottages. Nightlife is dancing at gay and lesbian bars, bingo at church, and performances by a range of talent from Wynton Marsalis to Lily Tomlin to the pop band Suede. You can mingle with the multitudes in the art galleries, shops, and restaurants along narrow streets in the heart of town, or you can escape to walk, swim, and sun on remote beaches, dunes, and forests of the Cape Cod National Seashore.

Created in 1961, the National Seashore preserves the Cape's natural splendor from Provincetown to Chatham along with its lighthouses, cranberry bogs, summer houses, and other human pursuits of happiness. About 5 million visitors a year come to this popular park.

This tour begins at the National Seashore's Province Lands Visitors Center. To get there take Route 6 to the traffic lights at Race Point Road, then turn right and go about 2 miles to the visitors center.

17 • Provincetown and North Truro

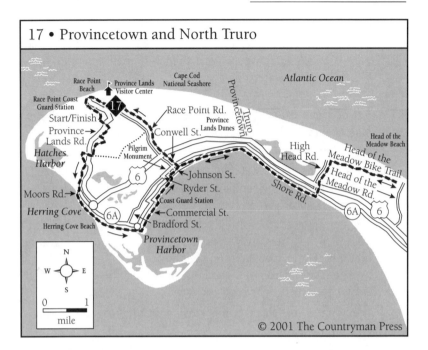

Race Point Beach
Province Lands Visitor Center
Race Point Coast Guard Station
Start/Finish
Province Lands Rd.
Hatches Harbor
Pilgrim Monument
Cape Cod National Seashore
Race Point Rd.
Province Lands Dunes
Conwell St.
Atlantic Ocean
Truro
Provincetown
Head of the Meadow Beach
High Head Rd.
Head of the Meadow Bike Trail
Head of the Meadow Rd.
Shore Rd.
Johnson St.
Ryder St.
Coast Guard Station
Moors Rd.
Herring Cove
Herring Cove Beach
Commercial St.
Bradford St.
Provincetown Harbor

N
W E
S
0   1
mile

© 2001 The Countryman Press

0.0 *Starting at the Province Lands Visitors Center, go down the hill to the amphitheater to take the paved bike trail to Race Point, named for the racing crosscurrents and riptides there. Watch out for windblown sand on the trails.*

Open daily from late spring to mid-October, the visitors center (508-487-1256) offers daily walks and talks in summer, a good gift shop, rest rooms, and a magnificent panoramic view of your travels.

0.6 *Stop and cross Race Point Road and turn right onto the bike trail to Race Point.*

Along the way you will cross the roads to Provincetown Municipal Airport, with its charter and sightseeing flights.

1.0 *At Race Point Beach there's a view of the Race Point Coast Guard Station to your left, a bathhouse straight ahead, and the Old Harbor Lifesaving Station, now a museum, to your right.*

Go to the overlook behind the bathhouse to see the beach, which is popular with anglers. The Race Point Lifesaving Station, built in 1872, was one of nine built on Cape Cod after Congress established the U.S. Lifesaving Service, the forerunner of the U.S. Coast Guard. Its sister station was barged here in 1977 from an eroding shore in Chatham.

1.6 *Retrace your route and veer right at the intersection onto the bike trail toward Herring Cove Beach, where once oil was extracted from herring and whales.*

2.0 *As you labor up a steep hill on the bike trail, distract yourself by noticing the Provincetown Pilgrim Monument behind the dune in front of you.*

The monument, 252 feet tall on a 100-foot-high hill, is a way to take your bearings anywhere on the Lower Cape. The granite monument, modeled after the bell tower of the Torre Del Mangia in Siena, commemorates the Pilgrims' arrival here, after which they moved on to look for a better harbor and source of water.

3.3 *Veer right at the intersection, staying on the bike trail toward Herring Cove.*

3.9 *This hilly trail leads through a glorious landscape of dunes that stops bicyclists in their tracks.*

Tall strands of beach grass, stunted scrub pines, and thickets of roses and beach plums help anchor the dunes. Dragonflies and small birds constantly dart in the air.

4.4 *Emerge into the Herring Cove parking lot.*

Cruise along the parking lot, just steps away from the beach. Watch out for speed bumps, surf casters, and strollers. This is a great place to whale-watch and people-watch. Pass in front of the snack bar and cycle to the other end of the parking lot. Look to your right and see Race Point Light, built in 1817 to guide mariners around this treacherous hook of land.

5.1 *Following the paved bike trail, emerge onto Moors Road and turn right. Moors Road becomes Route 6A.*

5.9 *Pass Bradford Street, which runs the length of Provincetown, and arrive at the traffic circle called the West End Rotary.*

Here is the site of First Landing Park, marking the Pilgrims' first landfall in the New World. The nearby Provincetown Inn is where heavyweight boxer Marvin Hagler once trained.

6.0 *Turn left onto Commercial Street, one-way for cars since 1932 but two-way for the town's many bicyclists.*

Enjoy the elegant gardens along the way and note the well-maintained homes; many are now inns and beds & breakfast for the town's visitors.

6.2 *A public parking lot provides a first good look at Provincetown Harbor and its dwindling fishing fleet.*

Birthplace to whaling and lobstering, Provincetown in the 1870s harbored as many as 300 ships during summer, when the seiners of the East Coast mackerel fleet anchored here. With 4,480 residents in 1885, Provincetown was the Cape's most populous town, home to netmakers, painters, blacksmiths, traders, boatbuilders, and fishermen. Now about 14 fishing boats make day trips to try to catch what's left of the once plentiful cod, yellowtail flounder, and other fish off these shores.

6.6 *Take the jog to your left around the U.S. Coast Guard Station.*

This is one of only four active stations still in service on Cape Cod. Here you are starting to enter Provincetown proper, with its many restaurants, art galleries, and summer shops.

Adams' Pharmacy is a year-round place to get a cup of coffee or a cherry cola at the soda fountain. In the summer, Mo-Jo's on the way to the wharf offers everything from fajitas to root beer floats at affordable prices. The Portuguese Bakery is a culinary detour to the mouthwatering fried bread and sweet loaves beloved by local residents. In the town's ever-changing restaurant scene, Napi's on Freeman Street is a reliable and special favorite for a drink or dinner.

7.3 *In the heart of Provincetown is the town hall. To continue the tour, turn left onto Ryder Street, then right onto Bradford Street.*

There are public rest rooms on the second floor of the town hall, built in 1880 on the old Ryder homestead. After that you'll pass the bas-relief Pilgrim Memorial. Follow Bradford Street, built in 1873, through town, past restored inns, guesthouses, and small markets.

There are two possible side trips at the junction of Ryder Street. You can turn right on Ryder Street to reach MacMillan Wharf, where there are rest rooms, whale-watching ships, fishing boats, and yachts. For another side trip, climb the stairs of the Provincetown Pilgrim Monument. To get there, turn left on Ryder Street and make an immediate left onto Bradford Street. Turn right onto Winslow Street, climbing a hill past the high school. Turn right into the parking lot. The museum is open 9–5 daily through November. To rejoin the tour, exit from the far end of the parking lot and coast down High Pile Road to Bradford Street, then turn left.

8.6 *Turn left onto Shore Road (Route 6A) at the flashing yellow light.*

9.5 *Enter Truro and its Beach Point village*

This narrow barrier beach is lined with cottages that are often painted and photographed by artists such as Joel Meyerowitz. Travel through the architectural garden of Day's Cottages; each cottage is named after a flower.

10.4 *Turn left toward Route 6. Turn left onto Route 6, then right onto High Head Road.*

This high plateau was created by the glacial deposits that eroded to create the flat outwash plain of Provincetown. Wind and waves still mold this land, eating away at the coastal bluffs and pushing the sand dunes a few feet a year to bury forests and nearby Pilgrim Lake.

10.8 *Veer right onto a dusty gravel road. It leads to the parking lot for the paved bike trail to Head of the Meadow Beach in Truro.*

11.2 *Pause at the Pilgrims' first sign of fresh water in the New World.*

Comb the hill for a view of the thickets they pushed through in their search for a habitable home. Provincetown is still short of drinking water supplies and imports water from Truro.

12.4 *The trail ends at Head of the Meadow Road. Turn left to the beach, another beautiful destination for a walk, a picnic, or a rest in the dunes.*

With a smile, these blue boxes trap greenhead flies each summer in a Provincetown marsh.

14.4 Retrace your route to the parking lot, down High Head Road to Shore Road, and back along Shore Road to the flashing yellow light at the entry to Provincetown's East End.

17.8 Veer left onto Commercial Street.

Ride slowly to enjoy the architectural details of the homes and the whimsy of the gardens squeezed into these small lots. In winter the same ride is stark and elegant, stripped to essentials.

18.9 Turn right onto Johnson Street, which leads to Bradford Street. Turn right onto Bradford, followed quickly by a left turn onto Conwell Street.

Just before you turn off Commercial Street onto Johnson Street, you'll pass the Provincetown Art Association and Museum, featuring local and international art since 1915. Just beyond the turn, in the 1860 Methodist church, is the town-owned museum, which displays art, whaling exhibits, and other local artifacts. Hours are 10–6.

153

19.3 *Cross Route 6 at the stoplight and continue straight onto Race Point Road.*

19.6 *At the recycling center, cross to the left of Race Point Road to the paved bike trail that leads to the Seashore's Beech Forest.*

19.8 *At the fork, turn right to continue to the visitors center. At the stoplight, cross Race Point Road into Provincetown's Wood End.*

Here you'll pass through shady groves of oaks and maples and briefly ride out onto exposed dunes. For a short side trip, turn left at the fork to the Beech Forest. This is one of the few surviving patches of forest that gave Wood End its name.

20.2 *Your tour ends where it began, at the Province Lands Visitors Center.*

Bicycle Repair Services

Black Duck Bike Shop, LeCount Hollow Rd., S. Wellfleet, MA 508-349-9801

Galeforce Bike Rentals, 144 Bradford St. Ext., Provincetown, MA 508-487-4849

Idle Times Bike Shop, Brackett Rd., N. Eastham, MA 508-255-8281

Little Capistrano Bike Shop, Route 6, Eastham, MA 508-255-6515

Nelson's Bike Shop, 43 Race Point Rd., Provincetown, MA 508-487-8849

Wellfleet Cycles, 54 E. Commercial Street, Wellfleet, MA 508-349-9322

. NANTUCKET

The Island of Nantucket

The name Nantucket, meaning "faraway isle," was given to the island by its first inhabitants, natives of the Paleo, Archaic, and Woodland periods. After the arrival of the Thomas Macy family in 1659, many English settlers came seeking religious freedom from the Puritanism that dominated the mainland. The island's first town, Sherburne, was incorporated in 1673 and was situated in what is now Madaket. While sheep raising established an early economic prosperity, by 1690 shore whaling became the island's major industry. By 1712 Nantucket whalers had turned to deeper waters, seeking the whale oil that was used for lighting until the Civil War. Despite its small size, Nantucket provided numerous jobs in the local boatbuilding and whaling industries.

The island's population fluctuated greatly during the whaling industry's upturns and downturns. By 1830, it ranked third in size and wealth among Massachusetts's seaports. Its population peaked at 9,700 in 1840, but by then the whaling industry had also peaked and was beginning to decline. Evidence of this early prosperity can still be seen in the extravagantly built old homes that line the streets of Nantucket Town.

Nantucket whaling finally came to a halt in 1870. Mainland competition, migrations west to California, and industrialization all contributed to its demise. Another major setback to the economy of the island was the Great Fire of 1846, which destroyed the wharves and more than a third of the town in and around Main Street. A great deal of whaling money was used to rebuild the downtown, as well as to invest in railroads, cotton mills, and banks on the mainland. Farming and fishing soon became the island's main businesses. The old sheep fields were used for cow pastures and to grow grain. Seafood was shipped off the island to supply major population centers on the mainland and was sold locally to guesthouses that were built to accommodate the increasing number of tourists. Nantucket was becoming the island resort it is today.

Nantucket has retained its whaling and architectural heritage through museums and organizations that protect historic landmarks. Nantucket now is fighting for a future as a thriving community and not simply a playground for the well-to-do. The island's latest economic threat is development and skyrocketing real estate prices. Houses now cover most landscapes. Island employers fly or ferry workers daily from the Cape to an island where few can afford to live.

Except for its cobblestones, the island is still hospitable to strangers. Routes to beaches are well marked by colored signs. The island's transit system can be a godsend for bicyclists. The buses can carry bicycles and riders who may be tired, out of time, or out of good weather. Most buses leave from Nantucket Center, near the famous Mileage Board that shows the distances from Nantucket to various places around the globe. This is indicative of how Nantucketers think—Nantucket is the center of the universe!

18

Around Nantucket Town and to Surfside

Distance: *10.7 miles*
Terrain: *Flat with two moderate climbs*

This tour begins in the town of Nantucket then heads south through the countryside to one of the island's popular beach areas, Surfside. At first the tour offers a glimpse of some of Nantucket's grander homes, then it winds through quaint, narrow streets where you'll see more modest homes nestled closely together. Both views of Nantucket Town are rich with history and offer scenic tours from the vantage point of a bicycle.

0.0 Beginning at the intersection of Main Street and Washington Street. Turn left at the famous Nantucket Mileage Board. Turn left at the next two corners and cross to Easy Street.

On your right will be Old South Wharf and then Straight Wharf. Old South Wharf is located just past the A&P supermarket. The wharf was constructed in 1760 and was one of the old whaling wharves. Today it's used to dock private yachts during the summer and has art galleries and retail shops running its length.

Straight Wharf extends "straight" to the water from the cobblestones of Main Street. Built by Thomas Macy in 1723, the wharf marks the origination of the whaling industry. It's now home to shops and restaurants and is the dock for the Hy-Line ferries. The Thomas Macy Warehouse on the right side of Straight Wharf once stored all the necessary gear used on the whaling ships. The warehouse is the setting for the Museum of Nantucket History, which illustrates Nantucket's geological beginnings and history from the days of whaling up through modern times.

0.1 The Club Car restaurant is on your left.

18 • Around Nantucket Town and to Surfside

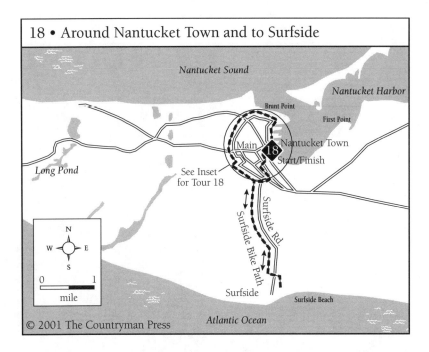

The restaurant's bar is housed in an actual railway car from the Nantucket railroad. The car was saved when the railway was abandoned during World War II.

Just a bit farther down on your right is the Old North Wharf, easily seen from the boat basin just past the wharf's entrance. It provides a look at the summer homes that were once simple fishing shacks, as well as a nice view of the harbor.

0.2 Turn left onto Broad Street.

A right turn here would bring you to Steamboat Wharf, where the ferry docks and unloads cars and trucks from the mainland. This site is also where the old railroad tracks began for the trip to Surfside and Siasconset.

0.3 Turn right onto South Beach.

On the corner here are the Peter Foulger Museum and the Nantucket Whaling Museum. Peter Foulger was Benjamin Franklin's grandfather, and this museum shows the life of the island through

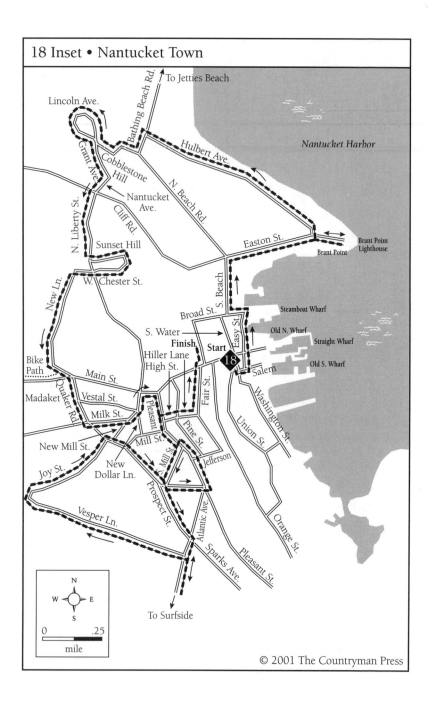

18 Inset • Nantucket Town

To Jetties Beach

Lincoln Ave.

Bathing Beach Rd.

Nantucket Harbor

Hulbert Ave.

Grant Ave.

Cobblestone Hill

N. Beach Rd.

Nantucket Ave.

N. Liberty St.

Cliff Rd.

Sunset Hill

Easton St.

Brant Point Lighthouse

Brant Point

New Ln.

W. Chester St.

S. Beach

Broad St.

Steamboat Wharf

S. Water

Easy St.

Old N. Wharf

Finish

Start

Straight Wharf

Bike Path

Hiller Lane

High St.

Old S. Wharf

Main St.

Salem

Fair St.

Madaket

Quaker Rd.

Vestal St.

Pleasant

Washington St.

Milk St.

Pine St.

Union St.

New Mill St.

Mill St.

S. Mills St.

Jefferson

Joy St.

New Dollar Ln.

Prospect St.

Atlantic Ave.

Orange St.

Vesper Ln.

Sparks Ave.

Pleasant St.

N
W E
S

To Surfside

0   .25
mile

© 2001 The Countryman Press

displays of furniture and other household items. Many whaling-family portraits are also on display.

The second floor of the Peter Foulger Museum is home to the Nantucket Historical Association's research center and the Edouard A. Stackpole Library. The library has an extensive collection of old ships' logs, diaries, genealogical charts, other published historical works, and more than 35,000 photographs that relate the history of maritime Nantucket.

The Nantucket Whaling Museum provides a look into the island's whaling history; every type of implement, from acquisition to processing gear, is in the collection. The museum also has a vast scrimshaw collection, traditional whaleboats, and even a 43-foot-long skeleton of a finback whale. A lecture on the history of whaling is offered three times a day. The building was originally the candle factory of Richard Mitchell.

On your right is the Nantucket Yacht Club.

0.4 *At the stop sign, turn right onto Easton Street.*

0.7 *The tour loops around to your left onto Hulbert Avenue. Continue straight ahead for a short detour to the Brant Point lighthouse.*

On your right is Nantucket's Coast Guard Station. If you continue onto the beach you'll see the present Brant Point lighthouse, smaller than the original and Nantucket's first lighthouse. After leaving the lighthouse, retrace your route and turn right onto Hulbert Avenue.

1.5 *Turn left onto Bathing Beach Road.*

For a short detour to Jetties Beach, turn right on Bathing Beach Road and go 0.2 mile. In the late 1800s, the federal government built stone jetties to keep an encroaching sandbar from closing Nantucket Harbor. At the beach you'll find bicycle racks, a playground, a restaurant, rest rooms, changing rooms, and showers. The surf is mild here and lifeguards are on duty.

1.6 *Turn right onto North Beach Street and then make an immediate left up Cobblestone Hill.*

The grade is steep, so you may want to walk your bike up the hill.

1.8 Take this short loop just for fun. At the top of the hill turn right onto Grant Avenue, which becomes Lincoln Avenue as it circles around. Three-quarters of the way around the circle you'll see the entrance to Steps Beach. Continue around the circle back to Grant Avenue. Follow this to the end and turn right onto Nantucket Avenue.

2.2 Using extreme caution, go straight across Cliff Road onto North Liberty Street.

2.5 Before reaching the stop sign, turn left up Sunset Hill.

On your left is a drive with a sign for Nantucket's oldest house, built in 1686. In fact, it's one of the oldest structures in the United States, the former home of Jethro Coffin and Mary Gardner, children of the two most influential families on the island. When the families were united by Jethro and Mary's marriage, each family made a contribution to the newlyweds' future home—the land was given by Captain John Gardner and the wood by Peter Coffin. The house offers a fine example of early post-and-beam construction and the minimal furnishings typical of that period.

2.6 At the bottom of Sunset Hill, turn right onto West Chester Street.

2.8 Go straight through the stop sign, then turn left onto New Lane.

3.2 Turn right in front of the flagpole. This is a busy intersection, so please use caution. You'll continue straight across to Quaker Road, past the Quaker cemetery on your right, then turn left onto Vestal Street.

On your left is the Old Gaol, or jail, built in 1805. It is a simple two-story log cabin built a little sturdier than most, with the inside divided into four cells. This type of jail is the oldest in Massachusetts. The last felon was held here in 1934.

Farther down on your left is the Maria Mitchell Association's offices, housed in the residence where Nantucket's celebrated scholar was born in 1818. At the young age of 29, Mitchell discovered a comet; she was the first woman given fellowship into the Academy of Arts and Sciences; and she was the first female

The Nantucket Mileage Board

professor of astronomy at Vassar College. The association runs a library across the street in the old schoolhouse where Mitchell's father taught celestial navigation to young whaling captains and their sisters. It contains Maria Mitchell's manuscripts and science books as well as contemporary journals of natural history and, of course, astronomy.

The association conducts nature and birding walks, wild-flower walks, natural science lectures, and nature classes for children. It also runs a small aquarium on Washington Street that houses a sampling of Nantucket's marine creatures.

3.5 Turn left onto Milk Street.

The road turns to brick and takes you around the Soldiers and Sailors Monument, which stands in memory of the Nantucketers who died in the Civil War.

3.6 Turn right down Main Street with its cobblestone surface.

On your left look for the "Three Bricks," brick homes built by Joseph Starbuck in 1838 for his three sons, George, Matthew, and William. Starbuck was a wealthy whale-oil merchant who withheld the deeds to the three homes until his sons reached 40 years of age—a successful attempt to keep them in the family business.

Opposite the Three Bricks stand the "Two Greeks," examples of Greek Revival architecture. The Two Greeks were built by another whale-oil merchant, William Hadwen. He built one for himself, the other for his daughter. William Hadwen's whale-oil factory is now the home of the Nantucket Whaling Museum on Broad Street, while his home is open to the public during the summer season.

3.7 *Turn right onto Pleasant Street, just before the Two Greeks.*

3.8 *Turn right onto South Mill Street, a gradual climb.*

At the top of South Mill Street is the Old Mill, built in 1745 by Nathan Wilbur. It survives four other wind-powered mills that stood with it on a range of hills, operating during Nantucket's farming era. Note that the wagon wheel attached to the top of the mill is used to rotate the sails into the wind. This Nantucket Historical Association property is open to the public in the summer season.

4.0 *Turn right at the top of the hill, then turn left onto Prospect Street. At the end of the street turn right onto Surfside Road.*

This is a busy intersection, so please use caution.

4.2 *Surfside Bike Path begins here.*

On your left are the high school and the community pool. Beyond that are playing fields and the entrance to the elementary school.

4.9 *The Shack snack bar is on your right.*

6.2 *Use caution—here the bike path crosses Surfside Road. In 0.2 mile you'll reach the entrance to Surfside Beach.*

Numerous bike racks are available, but these fill up quickly in the summer. Surfside Beach—with its food stands, lifeguards, public phone, rest rooms, and showers—is usually crowded during the summer season. The surf is moderate to heavy here.

If you continue to the end of Surfside Road, you'll come to Nantucket's original lifesaving station. It has since been converted into a youth hostel.

6.4 *Retrace your route from Surfside Beach back toward the center of Nantucket Town on the bike path.*

8.7 *At the end of the bike path, turn left onto Vesper Lane.*

On your right is the Nantucket Cottage Hospital.

9.3 *Turn right onto Joy Street.*

On either side of Joy Street is the Prospect Hill cemetery.

9.7 *Turn right onto Prospect Street. Go past New Mill, Mill, and North Mill Streets, then turn left onto South Mill Street by the old mill at the top of the hill. After making the turn, bear right and proceed down West York Street.*

10.0 *Turn left onto Pleasant Street opposite the African Meeting House.*

This is the island's only public building constructed and occupied by its free African American population, who have been part of the island's history since the 1700s. Originally a school, the 1827 building became a Baptist church and then a social center. It was bought in 1989 by the Museum of Afro-American History in Boston. Restored by 1999, the African Meeting House is now open to the public in summer.

10.1 *Turn right onto High Street, which becomes Hiller Lane after the intersection. At the end of Hiller Lane, turn left onto Fair Street.*

At the end of Hiller Lane, on your right, is the Woodbox Restaurant. Built in 1709, it's one of Nantucket's oldest buildings.

Look for St. Paul's Episcopal Church on the right side of Fair Street. This church was built of stone in 1901 and stands as a replacement for its predecessor, which was destroyed in the Great Fire. It was originally located on Broad Street next to the Jared Coffin House. Notice that the windows are Tiffany stained glass.

Opposite the church is the Nantucket Historical Association, in the Quaker Meeting House. The Meeting House, built in 1838, serves as a reminder of Quaker predominance on the island. It was used as a Quaker school for 55 years before becoming the headquarters for the Historical Association. Next to the Meeting House is the Fair Street Museum, which features changing exhibits.

10.5 *At the end of Fair Street, turn right onto Main Street.*

Here you'll see the Pacific Bank. It was established in 1818 and has been in service ever since. Maria Mitchell's father constructed the small observatory on the roof of the bank, from which she discovered the comet that made her famous.

10.7 Continuing in front of the bank down Centre Street, you'll come to the Jared Coffin House, the second of Mr. Coffin's mansions.

This one was located in town, where his wife believed she'd be happier than she would living on Pleasant Street. It resembles the Three Bricks, although Coffin intended it to be much more elegant.

This house marks the end of your tour. To return to the starting point, retrace your route down Centre Street, turn left onto Main Street, and follow it to the intersection with Washington Street.

Bicycle Repair Services

Young's Bicycle Shop, Steamboat Wharf, Nantucket, MA 508-228-1151

Other Bicycle Shops

Cook's Cycle Shop, 6 S. Beach Street, Nantucket, MA 508-228-0800
Holiday Bicycle, 4 Chester St. at Cliff Rd., Nantucket, MA 508-228-3644
Nantucket Bike Shop, Straight Wharf, Nantucket, MA 508-228-1999

19
Nantucket Town to Madaket

Distance: 19.3 miles
Terrain: Some challenging hills; paved and dirt paths

This tour winds through the town of Nantucket to the Cliff Road Bike Path. Along the route you'll get a good view of the majestic gray-shingled houses that overlook Nantucket Sound. You can take a side trip to Dionis Beach along fast-developing Eel Point Road or continue on the bike path to Madaket, situated at the western end of the island. On your return, you'll explore the cartpaths through Ram Pasture, Sanford Farm, and the Woods, 767 acres of moors, pastures, and woods preserved by the Nantucket Conservation Foundation and the island's Land Bank Commission.

You'll begin the tour at the eastern end of Main Street, where it intersects Washington Street. Notice the Pacific Bank as you look up Main Street; it will mark the end of the tour.

0.0 *Begin at the intersection of Main Street and Washington Street. Looking at the Mileage Board, turn left and turn left at the next two corners to cross to Easy Street.*

On your right will be Old South Wharf and then Straight Wharf. To ease the ride over the quaint but painful cobblestones, stand on your pedals.

0.1 *The Club Car restaurant is on your left. Just a bit farther down on your right is the Old North Wharf.*

0.2 *Turn left onto Broad Street, then in 0.1 mile turn right onto South Beach; on your right is the Nantucket Yacht Club.*

On the corner of Broad Street and South Beach are the Peter Foulger Museum and the Nantucket Whaling Museum.

19 • Nantucket Town to Madaket

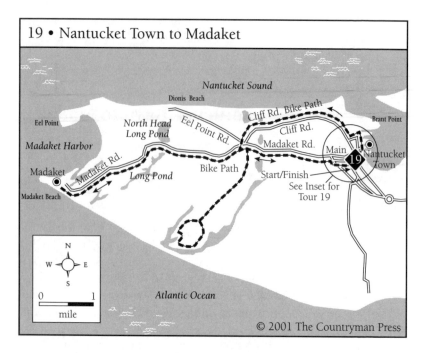

0.4 *At the stop sign, turn left onto Easton Street.*

0.6 *At the next stop sign, turn right onto Cliff Road.*

This scenic road is lined with some of the island's largest summer homes overlooking Nantucket Sound.

0.9 *On your left is Something Natural, a great place to stop for a snack or a packed lunch.*

1.7 *The Cliff Road Bike Path begins here, on the right. The terrain is quite hilly, with three large climbs.*

2.8 *Cross Eel Point Road. Turn left to cross Madaket Road carefully.*

Or, for a 1.8-mile side trip to Dionis Reach, turn right and take the bike path 0.7 mile to a large white rock. At the rock, turn right onto the bike path to the beach.

Dionis Beach is named after Dionis Coffin, who settled here in 1659 with her husband, Tristam. The town bought 2,400 feet of beach frontage here in 1954.

There are bike racks so you can lock up your bike, rest rooms, drinking water, and soda machines. Dionis is an expansive beach with sand dunes, mild surf, and lifeguards. Retrace your route to Eel Point Road and cross Madaket Road.

2.9 *Turn right onto the bike path.*

The bike path winds along—and at times away from—the Madaket Road. There are a few hills along this route, but no difficult climbs, and there are several rest areas at ponds.

5.0 *You'll see Long Pond on your left, with benches to sit on and ducks to watch.*

6.5 *You'll come to a small snack bar and the Westender Restaurant. From here continue 0.2 mile to reach the entrance to Madaket Beach.*

Bike racks are provided. The surf here is usually very heavy with a strong undertow. There are lifeguards on duty, but the only rest room is at the Westender Restaurant.

6.7 *Retrace your route back down the Madaket Road.*

10.5 *Go straight past the intersection of Eel Point and Cliff Roads.*

10.8 *Turn right to enter Sanford Farm, Ram Pasture, and the Woods. Go through the turnstile and pick up a map. You may need to lift your bike over the fence.*

This land offers an escape from the island's bustle as you explore the changing landscape of pastures, ponds, swamp, and farmland. There are 6.6 miles of paths open to the public for walking, biking, and horseback riding. There is an annual mountain-bike race along these challenging trails, through either bumpy grass, soft sand, or puddles.

If you take time to ride here, please keep in mind that this is conservation land. Please stay on the trails and try to leave no trace of your passing.

10.9 *Look to the left—you may see ospreys flying or sitting on their nesting platform.*

Also to the left is Waqutaquaib Pond, covered with water lilies in the summer. Look for blueberries as you pass by.

19 Inset • Nantucket Town

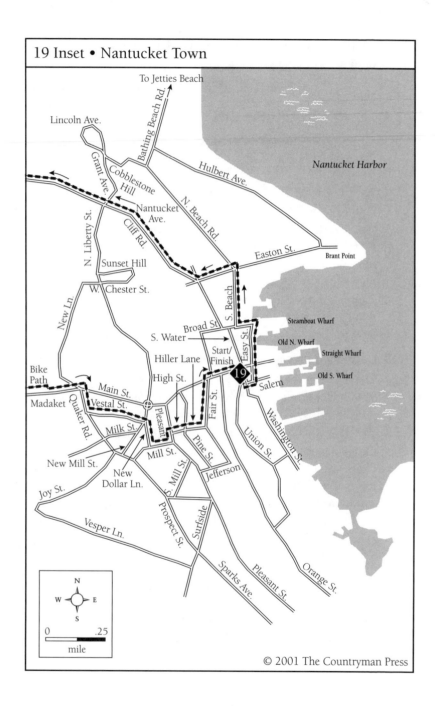

To Jetties Beach

Lincoln Ave.

Bathing Beach Rd.

Nantucket Harbor

Cobblestone Hill

Grant Ave.

Hulbert Ave.

Nantucket Ave.

N. Beach Rd.

Cliff Rd.

N. Liberty St.

Sunset Hill

Easton St.

Brant Point

W. Chester St.

New Ln.

S. Beach

Steamboat Wharf

Broad St.

S. Water

Easy St.

Old N. Wharf

Straight Wharf

Start/Finish

Hiller Lane

Old S. Wharf

High St.

Salem

Bike Path

Main St.

Fair St.

Madaket

Quaker Rd.

Vestal St.

Pleasant

Washington St.

Milk St.

Union St.

New Mill St.

Mill St.

Joy St.

New Dollar Ln.

Pine St.

S. Mill St.

Jefferson

Prospect St.

Surfside

Orange St.

Vesper Ln.

Pleasant St.

Sparks Ave.

N
W   E
S

0   .25
mile

© 2001 The Countryman Press

12.6 Enjoy the panoramic view from the barn to Hummock Pond.

13.1 Veer left at the split in the trail.

13.9 Bump through the moors to the pond. Head back toward the barn.

Look for shorebirds as you near the pond.

14.5 Turn right to complete the loop.

15.3 Pass the barn. Climb uphill.

16.9 Pass through the gate and turn right onto the bike path.

18.5 The bike path ends here. Turn right onto Quaker Road.

On your right is the Quaker Cemetery. The Quakers, or the Society of Friends, were the first to organize a congregation on the island of Nantucket. Mary Coffin Starbuck established the monthly meetings in 1708.

18.6 Turn left onto Vestal Street.

On your left is the Old Gaol, or jail. Farther down on your left is the Maria Mitchell Association.

18.8 Go straight across Milk Street to New Dollar Lane. At the end of the lane, turn left onto Mill Street, then left onto Pleasant Street, and then make a quick right onto High Street. High Street crosses Pine Street and becomes Hiller Lane.

19.2 Turn left onto Fair Street at the end of Hiller Lane.

On your right is the historic Woodbox Restaurant. You'll see St. Paul's Episcopal Church on your right and the Nantucket Historical Association on your left.

19.3 At the end of Fair Street, turn right onto Main Street.

The tour ends at the Pacific Bank. The bank was established in 1818, the year that the first steamboat crossed Nantucket Sound carrying 60 passengers.

Bicycle Repair Services

Young's Bicycle Shop, Steamboat Wharf, Nantucket, MA 508-228-1151

The Pacific Bank, at the top of Main Street, was established in 1818.

Other Bicycle Shops

Cook's Cycle Shop, 6 S. Beach Street, Nantucket, MA 508-228-0800
Holiday Bicycle, 4 Chester St. at Cliff Rd., Nantucket, MA 508-228-3644
Nantucket Bike Shop, Straight Wharf, Nantucket, MA 508-228-1999

20
Nantucket Town to Siasconset

Distance: *21.3 miles*
Terrain: *Flat to gently rolling*

This is the longest tour on the island, encompassing much of Nantucket's history and development. The Polpis Road will take you past Shimmo, once a Native American settlement; Polpis, an early Native American settlement that was later inhabited by the colonists for farms and then for mills and factories; and open moors, a cranberry bog, and Nantucket's second largest inland body of water, Sesachacha Pond. The ride continues out to the exquisite town of Siasconset on the southeastern coast of the island. The return trip follows Nantucket's state highway, Milestone Road, through woodlands and moors and past cranberry bogs. The vast Milestone Bog has been in continuous operation since 1865.

0.0 At the Nantucket Mileage Board head west, up Main Street.

0.1 Turn left onto Orange Street, which will end at a rotary in 1 mile.

On your right a little way up is the Unitarian Universalist Church, built in 1809. It wasn't until 1837, though, that it actually became Unitarian. It was founded by Congregationalists who became unhappy with the First Congregational Church you'll see later in the tour.

The Unitarian Universalist Church's gold tower is home to a Portuguese bell installed in 1815. The bell was rung by hand until 1957, when it became mechanized. The town clock was a gift given by William Hadwen in 1881.

The tall side windows were fitted in 1844. The church also houses the oldest American-built organ, a Goodrich organ that was brought to the island in 1831.

20 • Nantucket Town to Siasconset

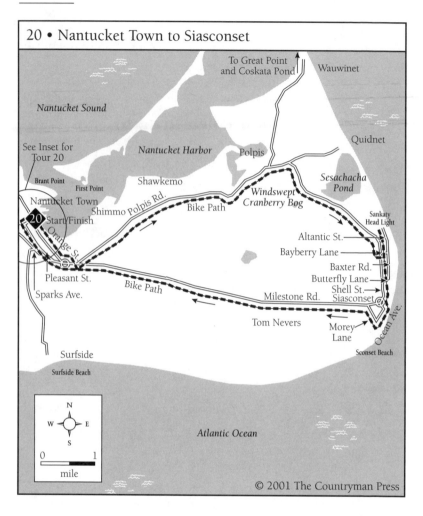

1.1 *Go around the rotary toward the Milestone Road Bike Path.*

The Milestone Road Bike Path (which you'll take on your return route) begins at this point. There's a water fountain here, a good opportunity to fill up your water bottles. To the right of the rotary you'll see the Rotary Restaurant. In front of the restaurant is the first milestone.

1.4 *Using caution, cross Milestone Road onto the bike path, 8.2 miles long, along Polpis Road.*

Along the right-hand side of the road you may catch glimpses of the moors. *Moor* is actually another name for "heathland." And the plants that grow best on moors are those in the heath family. They are well adapted to the wind, salt spray, and poor soil of Nantucket. They also regenerate much more quickly than other plants.

Heath plants became prolific on Nantucket through human activity. Native Americans cleared the land for crops by burning the fields. When Europeans arrived, they cleared the woods for pastures and fuel and they raised sheep, which ate the smaller trees and shrubs but mostly left the coarse heathers alone. With little competition or predation, the heath plants thrived. Today the moors are in danger because of the intrusion of woody plants and human development. Ways are currently being sought to preserve the heathlands.

2.1 *The road to Shimmo is on your left.*

3.4 *The road to Shawkemo is on your left.*

3.8 *The Lifesaving Museum is on your left.*

The museum building is a replica of a lifesaving station. An actual station is out near Surfside Beach. The museum tells of the perils of the seafaring life and describes the daring rescues undertaken by the lifesaving station's crew.

5.9 *The road on your left leads to Wauwinet.*

This road takes you out to the Wauwinet guest resort. From there you can reach Great Point and Coatue, wildlife preserves that are only accessible by foot or four-wheel-drive vehicle. Great Point excursions are available through the Trustees of Reservations. This area of Nantucket is a refuge for the island's vast array of shorebirds, including endangered species such as the piping plover and the roseate tern. In the salt marshes of Coskata Pond you may find great blue herons, osprey, snowy egrets, and whimbrels. Great Point has much to offer, even if you just want to witness the awesome power of the ocean.

6.1 *There is a cranberry bog on your right.*

Cranberries were first cultivated on Nantucket during the Depression years, when the whaling industry finally collapsed after its two-century domination. A large cranberry crop is still harvested

Susan Milton

A typical shingled cottage in Siasconset

annually on the island; most of the berries are sold to juice companies.

6.3 Pass the road to Quidnet.

7.5 Sesachacha Pond is on your left.

8.6 Sankaty Head Golf Course is on either side of the road.

9.2 Turn left onto Bayberry Lane. Turn left again at the end of the lane (you'll see a sign for Sankaty Head). In about 0.5 mile you'll come to Sankaty Head Light.

This lighthouse, built in 1849 on the eastern edge of the island, stands on a bluff 90 feet high. With a total height of 158 feet, its light carries 24 miles over the Atlantic Ocean. The lighthouse is endangered because the bluff it stands on is eroding. The views from here are magnificent.

10.0 Retrace your route to Bayberry Lane.

10.5 At the intersection with Bayberry Lane, continue straight on Atlantic Street. Atlantic Street becomes Baxter Road, then bears right to become Butterfly Lane.

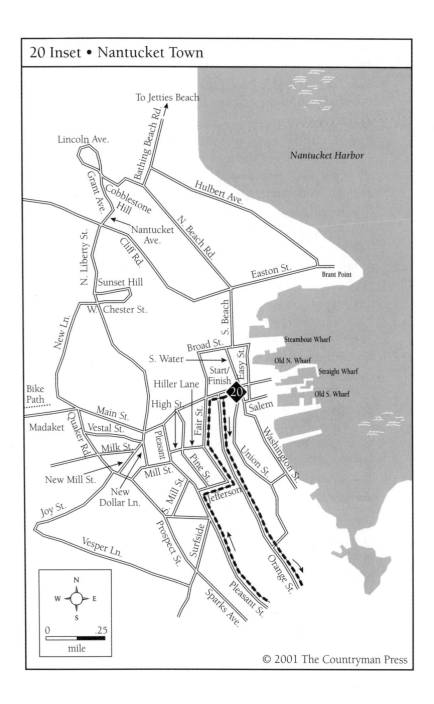

20 Inset • Nantucket Town

To Jetties Beach

Lincoln Ave.

Bathing Beach Rd.

Nantucket Harbor

Grant Ave.

Cobblestone Hill

Hulbert Ave.

Nantucket Ave.

N. Beach Rd

Cliff Rd.

N. Liberty St.

Easton St.

Brant Point

Sunset Hill

W. Chester St.

S. Beach

New Ln.

Steamboat Wharf

Broad St.

Easy St.

Old N. Wharf

Straight Wharf

S. Water

Start/Finish

Old S. Wharf

Bike Path

Hiller Lane

High St.

Salem

Madaket

Main St.

Fair St.

Pleasant

Washington St.

Quaker Rd.

Vestal St.

Milk St.

Pine St.

Union St.

New Mill St.

Mill St.

S. Mill St.

Joy St.

New Dollar Ln.

Jefferson

Vesper Ln.

Prospect St.

Surfside

Orange St.

Sparks Ave.

Pleasant St.

N
W—E
S

0   .25
mile

© 2001 The Countryman Press

Along this road are some lovely homes and great views of the Atlantic Ocean.

11.2 *Turn left onto Polpis Road (also called Sankaty Avenue here), then bear left at the Sconset sign onto Shell Street.*

11.5 *At the stop sign (there are public rest rooms here, on the right side of the road), continue straight until you run into Sconset Market and the post office. Circle around the post office and bear right onto Ocean Avenue. For a short detour, go past Ocean Avenue and proceed 0.2 mile to the beach.*

If you want to savor the slower pace of life here, you can leave your bicycle in the bike racks in back of the post office. As the bumper sticker says, 20 IS PLENTY IN SCONSET.

11.9 *At the stop sign on Ocean Avenue, turn right onto Morey Lane.*

Take time to explore this area where, during early summer, you can view the Siasconset roses. Climbing roses adorn numerous homes, trellises, and arbors on this island; climate and salt air provide a natural cure for many rose diseases.

12.3 *Turn left onto Milestone Road.*

On the journey down Milestone Road, look for the milestones. Six stones mark the 6 miles from the rotary. Look hard for the stone put up by a clever islander marking pi (roughly 3.14 miles).

The route is mostly flat and provides excellent views of the moors and bogs. Some of Nantucket's highest hills can be seen from the moors.

12.5 *The Milestone Road Bike Path begins on the left-hand side of the road.*

14.3 *On your right is an access road to the cranberry bogs.*

The road to the bogs is short and unpaved. Interior roads such as this one will take you through the moors, but you would need a map to prevent getting lost.

14.7 *Pass the entrance to Tom Nevers Road.*

18.7 *At the rotary, follow the signs for Madaket. At the fork in the road, keep right on Pleasant Street.*

19.4 *At the stop sign you'll notice the restored African Meeting House on the opposite right-hand corner.*

This small post-and-beam structure dates back to 1827, when its location was in a segregated community called New Guinea outside of town. The community welcomed slaves, freedmen, Native Americans, Quakers, Cape Verde Islanders, and abolitionists.

19.5 *Turn right onto Jefferson Lane. Go straight at the stop sign, then turn left onto Fair Street.*

On your left at the top of the hill is the Woodbox Restaurant. As you continue down Fair Street, you'll pass St. Paul's Episcopal Church on your right. Opposite that is the Nantucket Historical Association in the Quaker Meeting House. Next to the Meeting House is the Fair Street Museum, which features changing exhibits.

21.3 *At the end of Fair Street, turn right onto Main Street.*

The Pacific Bank marks the end of your tour.

Bicycle Repair Services

Young's Bicycle Shop, Steamboat Wharf, Nantucket, MA 508-228-1151

Other Bicycle Shops

Cook's Cycle Shop, 6 S. Beach Street, Nantucket, MA 508-228-0800

Holiday Bicycle, 4 Chester St. at Cliff Rd., Nantucket, MA 508-228-3644

Nantucket Bike Shop, Straight Wharf, Nantucket, MA 508-228-1999

MARTHA'S VINEYARD

Martha's Vineyard

Martha's Vineyard was named by English explorer Bartholomew Gosnold in 1602, either in honor of his daughter Martha; after his mother-in-law, who had partially financed his voyage; or in homage to a saint—historians are not quite sure.

"The Vineyard" is what modern-day explorers call the island, which, depending on their schedule, can be a day trip, a summer getaway, or a way of life. Only 15,000 people live year-round in the island's six towns. Summers, 102,000 live here. Thousands more arrive by ferry and airplanes for day trips, perhaps to take a quick bus tour or, too often, to risk life and limb on a moped, the island's leading cause of accidents.

The late Jacqueline Onassis bought an estate here near Gay Head. Television journalist Mike Wallace, humorist Art Buchwald, director Spike Lee, historian David McCullough, and political philosophers Robert McNamara and Lani Guinier are just a few of the thinkers and creators who have invested in this island getaway.

The Vineyard's original settlers, the Wampanoag tribe, called the island's western tip Aquinnah, "land under the hill." Gay Head was the name picked by English settlers after seeing its brightly colored cliffs. The Native American reservation on that section of the island was incorporated as a town in 1870 and renamed Aquinnah in 1997.

Martha's Vineyard is a place where people rally to save their general store, a gathering place for neighbors in search of coffee, Sunday newspapers, and a sense of community. That's why Alley's General Store in West Tisbury is owned by the Martha's Vineyard Preservation Trust, which leases the store to its current operators. And when local farmers needed a larger Agricultural Hall, volunteers offered their time and expertise to dismantle and reassemble a 1905 New Hampshire barn in West Tisbury.

The Vineyard is also a place where landowners donate major tracts of beach and moor to preserve them for future generations, and residents pay a tax on land transfers that goes into a fund to buy and preserve important pieces of land.

A few helpful hints: Most bicyclists rent bikes—$20 a day in 2000—

to travel the island between 8 AM and 6 PM. The best rate is weekly, at $75. There's no service charge for bicycle deliveries to Oak Bluffs or Vineyard Haven.

Please note that bicycling on sidewalks is banned on the island. When cycling, watch for the blue-and-white signs that point the way. In summer, most paths and roads carry a steady stream of bicyclists, so many that drivers are accustomed to watching out for them. Reciprocate, and the roads will be wide enough for everyone.

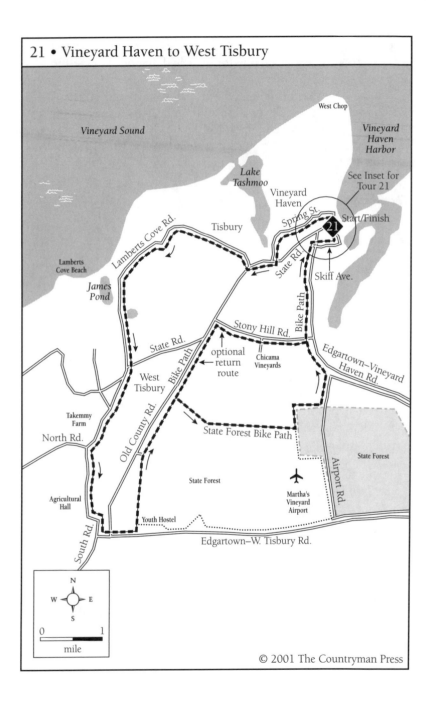

West Chop

Vineyard Sound

Vineyard Haven Harbor

Lake Tashmoo

Vineyard Haven

See Inset for Tour 21

Spring St.

Start/Finish

21

Tisbury

Lamberts Cove Rd.

State Rd.

Skiff Ave.

Bike Path

Lamberts Cove Beach

James Pond

Stony Hill Rd.

State Rd.

optional return route

Chicama Vineyards

Edgartown–Vineyard Haven Rd.

Bike Path

West Tisbury

Old County Rd.

Takemmy Farm

North Rd.

State Forest Bike Path

State Forest

State Forest

Airport Rd.

Agricultural Hall

Martha's Vineyard Airport

Youth Hostel

South Rd.

Edgartown–W. Tisbury Rd.

N
W · E
S

0   1
mile

© 2001 The Countryman Press

21
Vineyard Haven to West Tisbury

Distance: *19.3 miles*
Terrain: *Flat*

This tour is a quick way to get acquainted with Martha's Vineyard. It offers just a glimpse of harbors and bays, deep woods, shady roads, the studios of talented artisans, town centers, and wide open spaces.

Start the tour at the Steamship Authority's dock in Vineyard Haven.

0.0 *Go straight up Union Street, turn right onto Main Street, then turn left immediately onto Church Street.*

To your right is the Compass Bank, once a saddle shop and the suspected source of the 1883 fire that burned most of Vineyard Haven. To your left on Church Street is the Vineyard Playhouse, an 1833 meetinghouse. To your right is the Stone Church, a Methodist church built to replace a church that burned in 1922.

0.1 *Turn left onto Franklin Street.*

0.2 *Turn right onto Centre Street.*

0.3 *Turn left onto Pine Street.*

0.4 *Turn right onto Spring Street near the grammar school and playground. Stay to the right of the cemetery.*

1.5 *Turn right at the stop sign on State Road.*

1.6 *Stop at the overlook for a view of Lake Tashmoo.*

The road to your right, between the stone pillars, takes you down to the old waterworks and amphitheater. This spring-fed lake started serving as Vineyard Haven's source of drinking water in the late 1800s.

Lake Tashmoo was home to actress Katharine Cornell. Laurence Olivier and his first wife, Vivien Leigh, were among the friends who came to Chip Chop, Cornell's elegant home with its distinctive white chimneys. In 1995, television journalist Diane Sawyer and playwright Mike Nichols startled everybody by paying $5.3 million for the landmark, then the second-highest price ever paid for a property on the island. Such prices are ancient history now.

1.9 *Turn right onto Lamberts Cove Road.*

Jonathan Lambert was a carpenter who lived near the cove in the 1700s. Hundreds of spring bulbs and daylilies bloom here, across from the road's entrance, at the Vineyard Studio Gallery.

2.6 *Turn left onto John Hoff Road to find Ripley's Field Preserve, believe it or not.*

This 56-acre property, owned by the land bank, offers rides through open meadows, hills, and valleys.

Back on Lamberts Cove Road, you'll soon pass the Mary Wakeman Center, home to offices of most island conservation groups. Stop and look for maps.

5.0 *To your right is the entrance to Lamberts Cove Beach, a good place to sun and to swim in Vineyard Sound.*

5.3 *Lamberts Cove Inn is on your left.*

For a break, ride through pine groves to the 1790 inn and its gourmet restaurant.

6.0 *Pass James Pond on your right, a nice place for a quick swim or a rest.*

The pond was named after James, Duke of York, the owner of Martha's Vineyard until 1671.

6.9 *You're back at State Road. Turn right, following signs to Gay Head and Menemsha. You'll pass a grocery store, drugstore, and post office on your right.*

7.9 *Admire the horses at scenic Takemmy Farm.*

8.1 *Pass the shop of a glassblower in the yellow house on your right; it's open to visitors.*

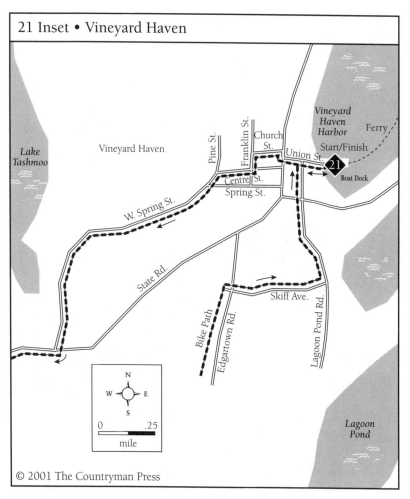

21 Inset • Vineyard Haven

Vineyard Haven Harbor

Vineyard Haven

Lake Tashmoo

Franklin St.

Pine St.

Church St.

Union St.

Ferry

Start/Finish

21

Boat Dock

Centre St.

Spring St.

W. Spring St.

State Rd.

Skiff Ave.

Lagoon Pond Rd.

Bike Path

Edgartown Rd.

Lagoon Pond

N
W E
S

0 .25
mile

© 2001 The Countryman Press

8.3 *Look for the landmark oak tree, photographed by Alfred Eisenstadt. Bear left onto South Road, toward West Tisbury and Gay Head.*

South Road was the Vineyard's first highway, along Wampanoag trails from Edgartown to the mill streams of Chilmark and West Tisbury.

8.7 *Stop by the Polly Hill Arboretum, a 60-acre private estate opened to the public in 1998. Its 20 cultivated acres are home to more than 2,000 species of plants and trees.*

Alley's General Store

9.1 *Pass Agricultural Hall on your right.*

The new hall is really an old post-and-beam barn, built in 1905 in New Hampshire. Rather than build a large, modern meeting hall, a crew of volunteers dismantled the barn and reassembled it here in West Tisbury in 1994.

This is the site of the Martha's Vineyard Agricultural Society's

Annual Livestock Show and Fair in August. In 1995, the new hall hosted a crowd-pleasing concert by Vineyard residents James Taylor and Carly Simon.

9.7 Pass the Old Parsonage Bed & Breakfast on your right.

9.8 Turn left onto the Edgartown–West Tisbury Road, following the signs to the Katama–Edgartown Road.

A detour to the right 0.1 mile would bring you to Alley's General Store and a chance to buy needed supplies and rest on its inviting front porch.

9.9 Pass Old Mill Pond, on your left.

The scene here is a real traffic-stopper, especially when the ducks and geese wander across the road. When the pond was known as Factory Pond, the nearby buildings made satinet, a fabric used for sailors' pea jackets.

10.0 Pass Old County Road on your left.

For an interesting detour, ride 0.4 mile down Old County Road to visit the Red Barn Gallery, which exhibits the marvelous photography of the late Alfred Eisenstadt and the very much alive Alison Shaw.

10.5 Turn left into the youth hostel and pick up the bike path, turning left toward Oak Bluffs.

The Manter Memorial Youth Hostel, which opened in 1955, was one of the first youth hostels in this country and is still one of the most popular.

You're now riding through Manuel E. Correllus State Forest, 4,400 acres in the heart of the island purchased between 1904 and 1914 by the state of Massachusetts. There are miles of bike paths and natural trails through these woods and meadows. The forest headquarters' number is 508-693-2540.

12.3 The bike path parallels Old County Road.

13.4 The bike path jogs to your right. Follow it to Airport Road, aka Barnes Road.

There's a bumpy return route to Vineyard Haven that brings you by an actual vineyard. This optional route is described at the end of this tour and adds just 0.9 mile to the ride.

15.9 *Turn left onto Airport Road.*

16.3 *At the blinking yellow light, turn left onto the bike path on the Edgartown–Vineyard Haven Road and head back to Vineyard Haven.*

17.9 *The bike path ends. Cross over to the right side of the road.*

18.3 *Turn right onto Skiff Avenue.*

18.8 *Turn left onto Lagoon Pond Road.*

> A barrier beach, spanned by a bridge, separates the pond from Vineyard Haven Harbor. The pond also is the site of a lobster hatchery established by the state in the 1950s, and of a shellfish hatchery established in 1980 that raises scallops and quahogs.

19.2 *Go straight at the chaotic intersection known as Five Corners, with the Black Dog Bakery on your right.*

19.3 *Return to the boat dock in Vineyard Haven where your tour began.*

> If you have time, check out the mural in the Steamship Authority's new terminal. Artist Margot Datz re-created the town's harbor and some of its people. She has illustrated four children's books written by singer Carly Simon.

Optional Route:

If you have a mountain or hybrid bike, you may wish to return over dirt roads by the Chicama Vineyards and Thimble Farm. The optional route starts at mile 13.4 of the main tour and from there goes as described below:

13.4 *When the bike path jogs to your right, continue straight on Old County Road.*

13.8 *Veer right onto State Road.*

14.3 *Turn right on Stony Hill Road, a potholed dirt road.*

15.3 *Chicama Vineyards are on your right.*

> The vineyard is open for tours and tastings Monday through Sat-

urday 11–5; Sunday 1–5. You can buy wines, jams, and salad dressings here.

15.7 *Pass the Thimble Farm, where you can pick your own straw-berries in season.*

17.4 *Turn left on Edgartown–Vineyard Haven Road, picking up the bike path at mile 16.3, and return to Vineyard Haven as described above.*

Bicycle Repair Services

Cycleworks, 105 State Road, Vineyard Haven, MA 508-693-6966

Wheel Happy, 8 South Water Street, Edgartown, MA 508-627-5928

Wheel Happy II, Beach Road, Edgartown, MA 508-627-3881

Other Bicycle Shops

DeBettencourt's Bike, Circuit Ave. Ext., Oak Bluffs, MA 508-693-0011

Martha's Bicycle, 4 Lagoon Pond Rd., Tisbury, MA 508-693-6593

Ride On Mopeds & Bikes, Lake Ave., Oak Bluffs, MA 508-693-2076

R. W. Cutler Bike Shop, 1 Main St., Edgartown, MA 508-627-4052

Sun and Fun, Lake Ave., Oak Bluffs, MA 508-693-5457

Vineyard Bike & Moped, Oak Bluffs Ave., Oak Bluffs, MA 508-693-6886

Island Sports, 7 Circuit Avenue, Oak Bluffs, MA 508-696-9311

22
West Tisbury, Chilmark, and Aquinnah

Distance: *25.2 miles (or 33.4 on alternate route)*
Terrain: *Some long, exposed inclines*

Park at Alley's General Store in West Tisbury: From Vineyard Haven, take State Road to West Tisbury, then turn left onto South Road. The store is 0.1 mile ahead on your right. There are bicycles for rent here, in back of the store. The town's council on aging is across the street.

0.0 Head south (turn right) onto South Road.

0.1 Pass the farmer's market on your right.

This is the new use for the old agricultural hall.

3.1 Actor John Belushi's gravesite is in the cemetery to your right.

Belushi's grave is within the rail fence visible from the road. Pilgrims leave beer bottles on the gravestone in homage to the hard-drinking Blues Brother. He is also the inspiration for toga parties here in his memory.

4.1 Pass the Allen Sheep and Wool Company on your right.

The wool company owners continue the tradition of these sheep commons by raising sheep. Wool blankets, sweaters, and yarn are sold in the shop.

5.1 Turn left, continuing on South Road toward Aquinnah.

This is called Beetlebung Corner, named for the grove of tupelo trees behind the rail fence. The hardwood tree's wood was used for beetles (or mallets) and bungs for casks. People planted tupelos in the 1700s to mark property lines.

Chilmark was home to the island's first governor, Thomas Mayhew. His English home was Tisbury. He named his island manor Chilmark, after a neighboring English town.

22 • West Tisbury, Chilmark, and Aquinnah

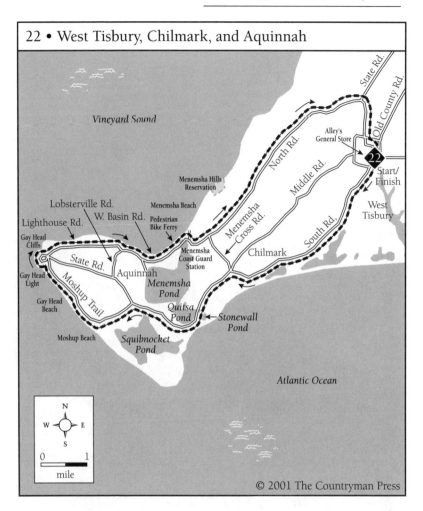

Vineyard Sound

State Rd.

Old County Rd.

North Rd.

Middle Rd.

Alley's General Store

22

Start/ Finish

West Tisbury

Menemsha Hills Reservation

Lobsterville Rd.

Menemsha Beach

W. Basin Rd.

Pedestrian Bike Ferry

Lighthouse Rd.

Gay Head Cliffs

State Rd.

Menemsha Coast Guard Station

Menemsha Cross Rd.

Chilmark

South Rd.

Gay Head Light

Aquinnah

Moshup Trail

Menemsha Pond

Gay Head Beach

Quitsa Pond

Stonewall Pond

Moshup Beach

Squibnocket Pond

Atlantic Ocean

N
W ◆ E
S

0   1
mile

© 2001 The Countryman Press

On your right you'll pass the Chilmark Store, reputed to have the island's best pizza. The next temptation is the Chilmark Chocolate Factory.

6.3 *Cross a bridge that overlooks scenic Stonewall Pond on your left and Quitsa Pond on your right, and head toward Menemsha Bight. The road narrows between stone walls in this hilly stretch.*

Susan Milton

The cliffs of Gay Head

7.2 *Stop here to gaze at incomparable views. Soon you'll enter the town of Aquinnah and cross the Squibnocket Herring Run, connecting Menemsha Pond and Squibnocket Pond.*

The views here are of Menemsha, the Chilmark woods, the shoreline and boats, and—on a clear day—the Elizabeth Islands, a string of island pearls that lead to Woods Hole. You can see why this is one of the most-photographed spots on the island.

8.5 *After a brief climb, turn left onto Moshup Trail.*

Moshup was the Wampanoags' legendary chieftain. The trail named for him presents sweeping panoramic views over dunes and heathlands to the sea. In 1995 the state of Massachusetts decided to buy 25 acres here as part of the island's effort to protect this vista. This is the only place on the 25-mile-long south shore where people can walk, drive, or bicycle for several miles with such views.

Jacqueline Onassis owned 200 acres on your left, between the road and sea, also a favorite place of her late son, John F. Kennedy Jr. Now his sister, Caroline Kennedy Schlossberg, maintains the family's estate here.

10.4 *Enjoy a fine view of Aquinnah and its lighthouse, built in 1798.*

In 1972, the Gay Head Wampanoag Tribal Council successfully sued the town of Gay Head for the return of 230 acres of its tribal lands, including the cliffs, now a major tourist attraction; the herring run; and the cranberry bogs off Lobsterville Road.

The tribe also wants to capitalize on its legal option to run gambling ventures. In 1995, the Gay Head Council and state of Massachusetts signed a contract for a $200 million casino in New Bedford as a way to generate money for the tribe and to create jobs for the mainland. That proposal is dead but the gambling idea is still a political hot potato among Wampanoags who question the tribe's direction and among mainlanders opposed to gambling.

11.1 *On your left, there's public access to the beach and a side view of the cliffs.*

The Martha's Vineyard Land Bank owns 420 feet of beach here.

11.5 *Turn left at the stop sign here to go to Gay Head Cliffs.*

You'll pass rest rooms on your way. Time your visit between tour buses, if you can.

11.7 *Stop at the cliffs' parking area and climb uphill to the overlook, past Wampanoag-run souvenir shops and restaurants with good chowder and other refreshments.*

Below you, waves crash into the steep-sided clay. Once 150 feet tall, the cliffs' height and colors—reds, browns, yellows, whites—have been diminished and muted by erosion. These cliffs were declared a national landmark in 1966.

In October, look for migrating hawks. The cliffs attract peregrine falcons, merlins, and kestrels, which swoop to catch the many smaller birds among the cliffs. Birders have also seen kettles of hawks—groups of 25 to 30 at a time.

11.9 *After your visit, return to the stop sign at the intersection of Moshup Trail and Lighthouse Road. Turn left onto Lighthouse Road.*

12.0 *The Outermost Inn is on your left.*

This inn is owned by Hugh Taylor, brother of singer-songwriter James Taylor. Notice the trees and shrubs, lush but stunted by wind and salt spray.

13.9 *Turn left onto Lobsterville Road.*

You'll ride past Lobsterville Beach, looking out on Menemsha Bight. In days past, lobstermen would summer here, building and getting their traps ready. Lobstering operations have now moved to safer anchorage in Menemsha.

14.7 *Turn left onto West Basin Road toward Menemsha Landing.*

On your left are the Aquinnah Cranberry Lands, 200 acres of dunes, barrier beach, natural cranberry bogs, and bird habitat.

For a short detour, go straight instead of turning onto West Basin Road. This brings you to a public landing on Menemsha Pond.

16.2 *Arrive at Menemsha Landing.*

Hugh Taylor runs the bike ferry here, which runs from May through mid-October. Just wait at the landing for the ferry to arrive. The price is $4–7.

When the ferry isn't running, take the alternate route described below, which adds 8.2 miles to this tour.

16.3 Disembark from the ferry and ride up the hill.

On your left is a wall of lobster buoys and a small, picturesque working harbor. On your right, pass the Homeport Restaurant, with fresh seafood available from its waterfront deck. In back of the restaurant looms the Menemsha Coast Guard Station.

16.4 Turn left onto Dutchers Dock Road.

16.5 The Bite, a pun on "bight," on your right serves fine clams and scallops.

16.7 Arrive at Menemsha Harbor and Beach.

Some of the island's best sunsets lure photographers here. Other visitors just enjoy swimming and sunbathing.

17.0 Ride back to the stop sign at North Road and turn left.

17.2 Pass the Menemsha Inn on your left.

Photographer Alfred Eisenstadt summered each year in these waterfront cottages and rooms until his death in 1995.

17.7 On your right you'll pass the Captain Flanders House and its windmill.

18.6 To your left is the Menemsha Hills Reservation & Beach, with nature trails through 210 acres of land.

The Trustees of Reservations own this land, with its trail to a rocky beach and its view of the Elizabeth Islands.

23.3 Turn right onto South Road, heading to West Tisbury and Aquinnah.

24.1 Pass the new Agricultural Hall on your right.

24.8 Turn right onto State Road.

24.9 Return to Alley's General Store on your right.

Across the road is the Field Gallery and sculptor Tom Malley's distinctive field of marblelike statues.

Alternate Route:

Take this alternate route when the Menemsha bike ferry is not running, starting at mile 16.2 at Menemsha Landing:

16.2 From Menemsha Landing, retrace your route along West Basin Road and then Lobsterville Road.

18.5 Bear left at the intersection with Lighthouse Road, staying on Lobsterville.

19.3 Turn left onto State Road, then veer left onto South Road at the intersection with Moshup Trail.

19.8 Turn right to visit the tribal headquarters of the Aquinnah Wampanoags, with a small yet growing museum.

23.1 Turn left onto Menemsha Cross Road. Pass the town hall on your right.

24.1 Turn left onto North Road.

24.6 Turn right on Dutchers Dock Road and rejoin the tour at mile 16.4.

Bicycle Repair Services

Cycleworks, 105 State Road, Vineyard Haven, MA 508-693-6966

Wheel Happy, 8 South Water Street, Edgartown, MA 508-627-5928

Wheel Happy II, Beach Road, Edgartown, MA 508-627-3881

Other Bicycle Shops

DeBettencourt's Bike, Circuit Ave. Ext., Oak Bluffs, MA 508-693-0011

Martha's Bicycle, 4 Lagoon Pond Rd., Tisbury, MA 508-693-6593

Ride On Mopeds & Bikes, Lake Ave., Oak Bluffs, MA 508-693-2076

R. W. Cutler Bike Shop, 1 Main St., Edgartown, MA 508-627-4052

Sun and Fun, Lake Ave., Oak Bluffs, MA 508-693-5457

Vineyard Bike & Moped, Oak Bluffs Ave., Oak Bluffs, MA 508-693-6886

Island Sports, 7 Circuit Avenue, Oak Bluffs, MA 508-696-9311

23
Vineyard Haven, Oak Bluffs, and Edgartown

Distance: *18.0 miles*
Terrain: *Some hills, mostly flat; at times exposed*

Memories of the island's northeast shore bring many visitors, from college students on vacation to summer people, back every year.

The tour starts in Vineyard Haven, a seaport cradled by two points, West Chop and East Chop. Vineyard Haven was once a whaling port; now the harbor welcomes ferry boats with freight and passengers and many yachts.

Oak Bluffs, the island's first summer resort, started as part of Edgartown, but in the mid-1800s it developed its own identity as the setting for annual summer campgrounds for churchgoers at Methodist revivals. The revivalists' tents were soon replaced by cottages that are now a tourist attraction, trimmed with intricate gingerbread and painted in many colors. Illumination Night each August is a spectacular time to wander through the campground, lit by Japanese lanterns.

Between Oak Bluffs and Edgartown is a beautiful bike path along the barrier beach between Nantucket Sound and Sengekontacket Pond, offering great views and places to stop and picnic.

The tour begins at the Steamship Authority's ferry dock in the town of Vineyard Haven.

0.0 *Turn left from the boat-dock parking lot.*

0.1 *Turn left onto Beach Road at the Five Corners intersection.*

You'll pass the Black Dog Bakery on your left (open 5:30 AM to 3 PM daily) and a bagelry and deli.

1.1 *Cross the drawbridge over Lagoon Pond and enter Oak Bluffs.*

To your left is the Eastville Point Beach, a delightful swimming and

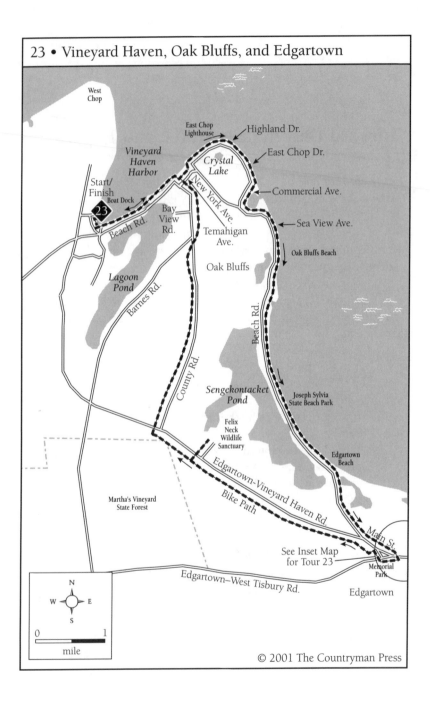

West Chop

Vineyard Haven Harbor

East Chop Lighthouse

Highland Dr.

East Chop Dr.

Crystal Lake

Commercial Ave.

Start/ Finish

Boat Dock

New York Ave.

Sea View Ave.

Beach Rd.

Bay View Rd.

Temahigan Ave.

Oak Bluffs

Oak Bluffs Beach

Lagoon Pond

Barnes Rd.

Beach Rd.

County Rd.

Sengekontacket Pond

Joseph Sylvia State Beach Park

Felix Neck Wildlife Sanctuary

Edgartown Beach

Edgartown–Vineyard Haven Rd.

Bike Path

Martha's Vineyard State Forest

Main St.

See Inset Map for Tour 23

Memorial Park

Edgartown–West Tisbury Rd.

Edgartown

N
W E
S

0   1
mile

© 2001 The Countryman Press

picnic stop. Look out in the harbor to see the *Shenendoah*, the three-masted schooner that sails on week-long windjammer cruises. To your right is Martha's Vineyard Hospital.

1.5 Turn left onto Temahigan Avenue. You'll soon pass the state police barracks on your right.

1.8 Turn left toward East Chop Lighthouse at the sign. The road becomes Highland Drive as it curves around East Chop.

This is the scenic route. Crystal Lake on your right was a prime source of ice, cut and stored for summer use.

2.5 Pass East Chop Lighthouse on your left.

You now overlook Nantucket Sound and, on a clear day, Cape Cod. Some say that in the 16th century the term *chop* meant a division of land.

3.2 As you coast downhill, pass the East Chop Beach Club on your left, overlooking Oak Bluffs Harbor. The road becomes East Chop Drive then veers right and becomes Commercial Avenue.

Start looking for the verandas and colorful houses with fancy gingerbread trim so characteristic of Oak Bluffs. You'll probably be tempted to climb on a porch and start rocking.

3.6 Turn left onto New York Avenue, going around Oak Bluffs Harbor.

You'll pass Our Market, which sells liquor and fast food. Oak Bluffs and Edgartown are the only island towns where you can buy liquor. The rest are dry.

On your right is the Wesley Hotel, built in 1879 and most recently renovated in 1986, the last of the large hotels so popular in the late 1800s, when Oak Bluffs was known as Cottage City.

3.8 Pass the famous Methodist Campgrounds on your right. On your left is the Surfside, selling food, drink, and gifts.

In August 1835, only a few people pitched their tents among the oaks for a week. Fifty years later, more than 1,000 tents and "wooden tents" (in the Carpenter Gothic style) were here.

The campground's open-air auditorium in central Trinity Park seats 3000 or more. Near the park is the Cottage Museum, open in summer Monday through Saturday 10:30–3:30.

3.9 On your left, pass the 1876 Flying Horses carousel.

With 22 wooden horses, this National Historic Landmark is the oldest operating merry-go-round in the United States. Obviously, the Methodist campers did more than worship.

4.0 Turn right onto Sea View Avenue.

4.1 To your right you'll pass Ocean Park and the bandstand. In 0.3 mile, Sea View Avenue becomes Beach Road; take the bike path that appears on your right.

This is the site of popular band concerts on summer nights and of the annual Oak Bluffs Fourth of July fireworks display. A short distance away, on your right, is the Farm Neck Golf Course, where then-president Clinton and Vernon Jordan, among others, liked to play golf.

5.7 The VFW Memorial Bridge marks the beginning of the Joseph Sylvia State Beach, which has a refreshment stand.

State Beach, open seasonally, is named after a former state representative who served the island from 1936 to 1966.

7.0 Cross the Edgartown Bridge, where the movie Jaws was filmed.

The crew of *Jaws* built the set on this narrow beach, which looked much wider in the film. To your right is Sengekontacket Pond, a 5-mile saltwater marsh estuary and source of fish and shellfish.

7.9 To your left is Edgartown Beach.

8.9 The Edgartown–Vineyard Haven road comes in from your right and becomes Main Street. Continue straight on Main Street toward the center of Edgartown.

The Square Rigger Restaurant presides over this junction, locally known as the Triangle. Amid the shops here is a pharmacy. The Dairy Queen is a must stop for locals.

9.2 To your right is the bike shop Wheel Happy II.

9.4 On your right is Memorial Park (locally known as Cannonball Park).

Should you want to shop and sightsee in Edgartown, proceed down Main Street and turn left onto Church Street to Pease Point

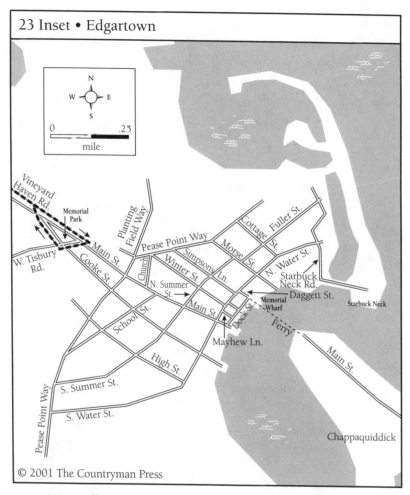

23 Inset • Edgartown

© 2001 The Countryman Press

Way. Follow the curve in the road to reach the bike racks. Lock your bikes and enjoy the town, very crowded in summer. Take your time walking or biking up and down the side streets, admiring the colorful doors, window boxes, and gardens in front of the century-old houses, built in the prosperous days of whaling and trade.

9.5 Circle Memorial Park to head out of town the way you entered.

A gingerbread cottage in Oak Bluffs

10.0 Pick up the bike path to the Triangle. Veer left onto the bike path to the Edgartown–Vineyard Haven Road to return to Vineyard Haven.

12.1 Pass the Felix Neck Wildlife Sanctuary on your right.

Or detour on the bike path and ride 0.6 mile to the sanctuary's parking area and trails to Sengekontacket Pond.

Both adults and children can enjoy the museum and nature trails here, owned by the Massachusetts Audubon Society.

The neck was named after the last Native American to live here in the 1700s. The property overlooks the pond, which is usually teeming with birds; from the duck blind you can watch the fowl from the water's edge. The sanctuary is open to the public year-round (508-627-4850).

13.2 Turn right on County Road, after passing Mahoney's Nursery and crossing to the bike path.

14.6 To your right, you'll pass the other side of the Farm Neck Golf Course.

You'll also pass the 71.8 acres of the Trade Wind Fields Preserve, open plains that were home to Wampanoags and African Americans for most of the 1800s. Within the preserve's boundaries is Pulpit Rock, the historic natural church of Rev. John Saunders, a Methodist minister here.

15.4 Pass by the intersection of Barnes Road and Wing Road. Cross to the bike path near the fire station.

The Trade Wind Fields Preserve is a rare sand plains habitat, preferred by unusual wildflowers and insects. This habitat exists here because of the land's use for years as a landing strip. To try out landings of your own on the trails, take a right on Wing Road, ride 0.2 mile. Turn right onto Pheasant Lane and, at its end, left on Meadow Way. At Trade Wind Road, turn right to find the driveway.

15.8 Pass by Bay View Road on the left.

Civil rights leader Martin Luther King Jr. vacationed on this road, near Lagoon Pond.

16.3 County Road ends. Turn left onto Eastville Road.

Pass by the island's hospital.

16.5 Eastville Road ends. Turn left onto Beach Road.

18.0 Return to the boat-dock parking lot.

Bicycle Repair Services

Cycleworks, 105 State Road, Vineyard Haven, MA 508-693-6966

Wheel Happy, 8 South Water Street, Edgartown, MA 508-627-5928

Wheel Happy II, Beach Road, Edgartown, MA 508-627-3881

Other Bicycle Shops

DeBettencourt's Bike, Circuit Ave. Ext., Oak Bluffs, MA 508-693-0011

Martha's Bicycle, 4 Lagoon Pond Rd., Tisbury, MA 508-693-6593

Ride On Mopeds & Bikes, Lake Ave., Oak Bluffs, MA 508-693-2076

R. W. Cutler Bike Shop, 1 Main St., Edgartown, MA 508-627-4052

Sun and Fun, Lake Ave., Oak Bluffs, MA 508-693-5457

Vineyard Bike & Moped, Oak Bluffs Ave., Oak Bluffs, MA 508-693-6886

Island Sports, 7 Circuit Avenue, Oak Bluffs, MA 508-696-9311

24
Around Edgartown and to South Beach

Distance: *10.4 miles*
Terrain: *Flat, sheltered*

Who was Edgar? He was the four-year-old son of the powerful duke of York. Edgar never knew about his town; he died before Thomas Mayhew, not knowing of Edgar's death, borrowed his name in 1671 to flatter his father.

Edgartown has always been the seat of Dukes County, named after the same duke. By the time Dukes County was created in 1683 by the New York Assembly, there already was a Kings County and a Queens County in Brooklyn and on Long Island. Later, Massachusetts won the rights to the island, which was also desired by the Dutch.

Edgartown was once world famous as home port to whalers and merchant captains who sailed all over the world. Their prosperity is reflected here in their homes, rich in architectural details of the Greek Revival and Federal styles.

Now their houses are elegant inns, art galleries, shops, and offices. The sailing ships that once filled the harbor have now been replaced by yachts, ferries, and whale-watching boats. And the island's economy depends on the preservation of its historic charm and accommodations for tourists. Indeed, Edgartown's streets fill with tourists every summer. The most famous tourists in the 1990s were Bill and Hillary Clinton, who relaxed with the island's summer people, such as Walter Cronkite, Mary Steenburgen and Ted Danson, Katharine Graham, Vernon Jordan, Patricia Neal, and Art Buchwald.

Bicycling along Edgartown's narrow streets is a slow affair in summer because of the throngs, and because you'll want to gawk at the scenery and people. Keep in mind that bicycling on sidewalks is banned on the island.

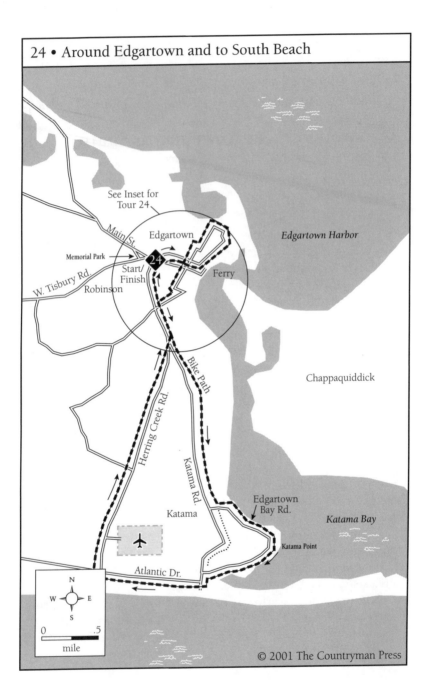

See Inset for
Tour 24

Main St.

Edgartown

Edgartown Harbor

Memorial Park

W. Tisbury Rd.

Start/
Finish

Ferry

Robinson

Chappaquiddick

Bike Path

Herring Creek Rd.

Katama Rd.

Edgartown
Bay Rd.

Katama Bay

Katama

Katama Point

Atlantic Dr.

N
W   E
S

0   .5
mile

© 2001 The Countryman Press

Start your tour at Memorial Park (locally known as Cannonball Park) in Edgartown.

0.0 *Go east down Main Street, as the cannon is pointing.*

0.2 *Turn left onto Pease Point Way. Follow signs to the bike path.*

The Pease family were early settlers in Edgartown, some say the earliest.

0.3 *Bike racks are available here if you want to explore along Edgartown's brick sidewalks. It's wise to lock your bike while sightseeing.*

Everywhere you turn, there's a postcard view of white clapboard captains' houses, picket fences, green grass, colorful window boxes and doors, and charming gardens.

Walk to your right to Church Street. There's a visitors center here with island information. Rest rooms are available.

Walk down Winter Street to the dock area and Memorial Wharf, a great place to watch for celebrities, their yachts and sailboats, and the ferry to Chappaquiddick. Don't miss the view from the wharf's observation deck.

0.4 *Continuing on the tour, turn right onto Simpsons Lane.*

0.6 *Turn left onto North Water Street.*

This street is lined with sea captains' homes that date from the whaling days in the 18th century. Pick out the Greek Revival- and Federal-style houses with fluted columns and pilasters. Look up at their widow's walks.

0.9 *Pass the Harbor View Hotel on your left and the lighthouse on Starbuck Neck to your right. Continue around the bend on Starbuck Neck Road to Fuller Street.*

1.1 *Turn right onto Fuller Street, traveling east to the sea. Return and head west on Fuller Street.*

Lighthouse Beach is an excellent beach for resting, sunning, or swimming.

1.4 *At the stop sign, cross Cottage Street.*

1.5 *Turn right onto Morse Street. Take the next left onto North Summer Street.*

1.7 *Continue through the stop sign at Winter Street, then continue across Main Street to South Summer Street.*

Admire St. Andrew's Church on your right, with its stained-glass windows by Louis Tiffany himself. The church, built in 1899, also has a dory bow for its pulpit, taken from the *Northern Lights*, a large schooner that sailed out of Edgartown Harbor for many years.

In the next block you'll find the Benjamin Smith House on your right. Built in 1869, the house is now the office of the *Vineyard Gazette*, which wonderfully captures the Vineyard's way of life while reporting the news.

1.8 *Next, pass the Charlotte Inn on your left, followed by the Federated Church, built in 1828 for the island's oldest congregation, first gathered in 1642.*

If you take a right here onto Cooke Street, you'll find the Vineyard Museum, also known as the Mariner's Museum. Take a good look at the house, built in 1765 for Thomas Cooke by ships' carpenters. The house's four corners slant away from the central chimney, just as a ship's decks slant away from the mast.

There are exhibits about the island's maritime history, its changing landscape, and the whaling industry. In summer the museum is open 10–4:30 daily; after Labor Day hours are 1–4 Wednesday through Friday, 10–4 Saturday. Call the museum for more information: 508-627-4441.

2.1 *Turn left onto High Street, then right onto South Water Street. Proceed to the four-way stop.*

2.4 *Turn left onto Katama Road. You'll soon see a bike path on your left. Turn onto the bike path heading toward South Beach.*

As the legend goes, a Native maiden named Katama and a chief named Mattakeeset fell in love, which so angered hostile warriors of the tribe that the couple swam out to sea and drowned.

Katama Bay now is the estuary contained by Chappaquiddick, South Beach, and Edgartown, with a narrow inlet through Edgartown Harbor.

4.9 *Turn left onto Edgartown Bay Road, leaving the bike path.*

24 Inset • Edgartown

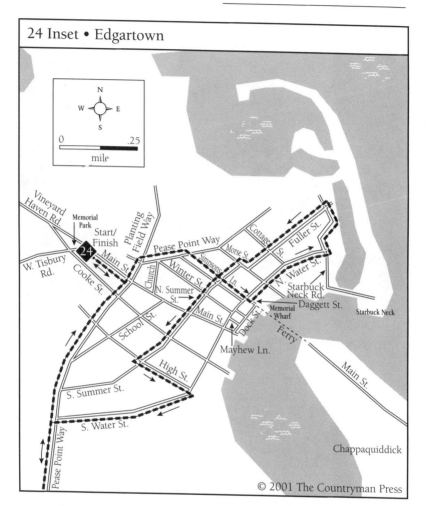

© 2001 The Countryman Press

This is a scenic mini-loop along the bay to Katama Point.

5.7 *To your left, the state boat ramp opens a window on Katama Bay and the barrier beach on the Atlantic Ocean.*

6.3 *Turn left onto Katama Road.*

South Beach, straight ahead, is very popular with the college crowd and other swimmers. There's great surf here.

6.4 *After visiting South Beach, turn left onto Atlantic Drive.*

Edgartown Harbor

7.3 *Turn right onto Herring Creek Road.*

There's a grass airfield to your right. People from the mainland fly down for day trips to South Beach. The Nature Conservancy manages the air park, 123 acres of sand plain. This is part of the Great Katama Plains, a special habitat.

8.2 *You may want to land at the diner at the airfield.*

Plane View, aka Mel's Diner, serves excellent breakfasts and lunches.

9.5 *At the stop sign, turn left onto Katama Road, toward Edgartown. Katama Road soon becomes Pease Point Way. Stay on Pease Point Way until the intersection with Main Street.*

Look for llamas at the estate of Ernie "Come on Down" Boch, famous for sales pitches for his cars and trucks on local television.

10.2 *Turn left at the stop sign onto Main Street, near the flagpole.*

10.4 *End at Memorial Park, where your tour began.*

Bicycle Repair Services

Cycleworks, 105 State Road, Vineyard Haven, MA 508-693-6966

Wheel Happy, 8 South Water Street, Edgartown, MA 508-627-5928

Wheel Happy II, Beach Road, Edgartown, MA 508-627 3881

Other Bicycle Shops

DeBettencourt's Bike, Circuit Ave. Ext., Oak Bluffs, MA 508-693-0011

Martha's Bicycle, 4 Lagoon Pond Rd., Tisbury, MA 508-693-6593

Ride On Mopeds & Bikes, Lake Ave., Oak Bluffs, MA 508-693-2076

R. W. Cutler Bike Shop, 1 Main St., Edgartown, MA 508-627-4052

Sun and Fun, Lake Ave., Oak Bluffs, MA 508-693-5457

Vineyard Bike & Moped, Oak Bluffs Ave., Oak Bluffs, MA 508-693-6886

Island Sports, 7 Circuit Avenue, Oak Bluffs, MA 508-696-9311

25
Edgartown to Chappaquiddick

Distance: *11.2 miles*
Terrain: *Flat; partially exposed*

As this tour takes you past whaling captains' houses and along narrow New England streets, past a busy harbor and scenic beaches, and over serene moors, you're likely to succumb to a rich sense of place that is all too rare a commodity in today's world.

This tour leaves Edgartown for a trip to Chappaquiddick Island, infamous forever as the site of Senator Edward Kennedy's car accident that killed a campaign worker. The well-preserved island deserves far better fame for its unspoiled open spaces, wildlife sanctuaries, and beaches. The big debate here today is over whether anglers should have unlimited vehicular access to fishing grounds on barrier beaches, or whether they must wait for endangered piping plovers to hatch and fly away.

Start the tour from Memorial Park (also known as Cannonball Park). Parking is at a premium in Edgartown. One solution is to avoid the center of town, park south of the Triangle, off the Edgartown–Vineyard Haven Road, and ride to the tour's start. Remember: Bicycling on Edgartown's brick sidewalks is prohibited.

0.0 Leave Memorial Park, riding east on Main Street.

Across the street from the cannonballs is the Martha's Vineyard Land Bank Commission office. The island levies a 2 percent tax on land transfers to create a fund to buy and preserve land. The Land Bank now owns 42 properties and also makes available a map of its conservation lands (508-627-7141).

0.2 Turn left on Pease Point Way. Follow signs to the Chappaquiddick Ferry and bike path.

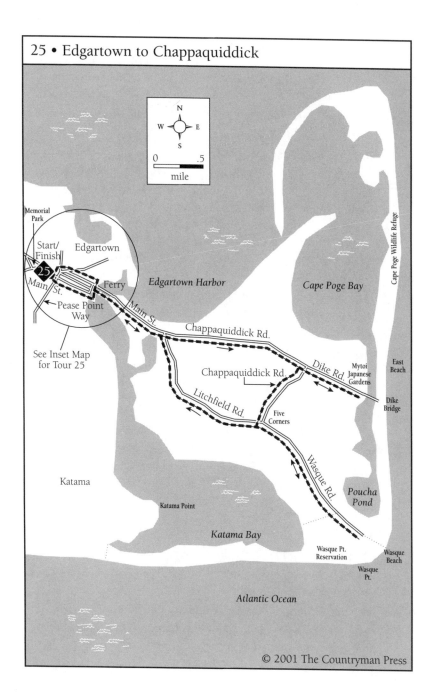

N
W   E
S

0   .5
mile

Memorial Park

Start/ Finish

Edgartown

25

Main St.

Ferry

Edgartown Harbor

Cape Poge Bay

Cape Poge Wildlife Refuge

Pease Point Way

See Inset Map for Tour 25

Main St.

Chappaquiddick Rd.

Chappaquiddick Rd.

Dike Rd.

Mytoi Japanese Gardens

East Beach

Litchfield Rd.

Five Corners

Dike Bridge

Katama

Wasque Rd.

Poucha Pond

Katama Point

Katama Bay

Wasque Pt. Reservation

Wasque Pt.

Wasque Beach

Atlantic Ocean

© 2001 The Countryman Press

For a short detour, where the road veers right, go straight on Planting Field Way to find, on your right, Sheriff's Meadow. Famous Vineyard journalist Henry Beetle Hough and Elizabeth Hough, his wife, turned Eel Pond into a 16-acre nature preserve.

0.4 *Turn right onto Simpsons Lane and pass the Shiretown Inn on your right.*

0.6 *Turn left onto North Water Street. After the ferry sign, turn right immediately onto Daggett Street. Ride to the ferry landing.*

You're on Memorial Wharf, a wonderful place to watch people and nature. Amid the shops, notice the Whale's Tail sculpture, installed in 1995. Climb to the observation platform for a great view of the harbor. To your left is Starbuck and its lighthouse. Straight across is Chappaquiddick Island and its ferries. To your right is the harbor, rimmed with houses.

0.7 *Take the On-Time Ferry to Chappaquiddick. Disembark and ride straight ahead on Main Street, which becomes Chappaquiddick Road.*

Welcome to Chappaquiddick, "Chappy" to locals. The two ferries are always on time because they run continuously, with only short breaks for meals in the winter. The fee for the 3-minute ride is $4 for a bike and rider, round-trip (call 508-627-9794).

First set aside as a reservation for about 100 Native Americans, the island soon became desirable to European settlers. By the end of the 1800s, only seven Native American descendants remained.

Now much of the island is preserved in state or private wildlife sanctuaries or beaches. In 1959, the Trustees of Reservations, a nonprofit conservation group, set aside 391 acres as a wildlife preserve. By 1995, there were 516 acres in the Cape Poge Wildlife Refuge, named after the barrier beach at the island's east end.

1.0 *Pass the Chappaquiddick Beach and Tennis Club on your left.*

The Chappy General Store, on the left, is a good place to stop in the summer.

2.3 *Pass the Chappaquiddick Community Center on your right.*

3.2 *Continue straight down unpaved Dike Road, following signs to Mytoi.*

25 Inset • Edgartown

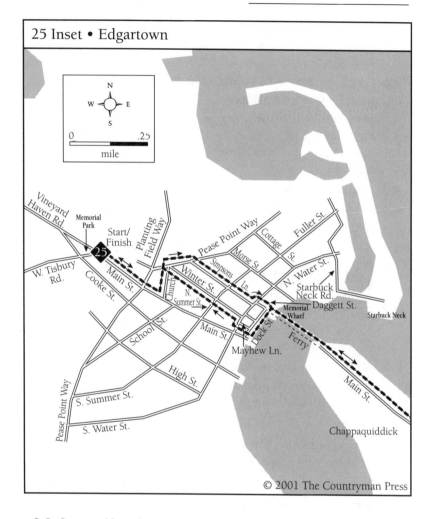

© 2001 The Countryman Press

3.5 *Stop at Mytoi Japanese Gardens on your left.*

This 14-acre property was donated to the Trustees of Reservations in 1958 by Mrs. Mary Wakeman.

Lock your bicycle in the rack provided. Walk around or have a quiet lunch amid the elegant shrubs and greenery or walk half a mile to the salt marsh and Poucha Pond.

The Trustees' guided tours, by oversand vehicles and canoes, leave from here and go to the Cape Poge Wildlife Refuge and lighthouse. Call 508-627-3599 for reservations and costs. More information is available at www.thetrustees.org.

3.8 Continue down the dirt road and stop at the famous Dike Bridge on Chappaquiddick.

Mary Jo Kopechne died after the car she was in, driven by Senator Edward Kennedy, went off the road and plunged into the water at this bridge to East Beach, the 5-mile-long barrier beach. Kennedy had made the wrong turn on his way to the Edgartown ferry.

4.2 Return down the dirt road toward Mytoi Gardens.

4.5 At the stop sign, turn left on Chappaquiddick Road (aka School Road) toward Wasque Reservation.

5.4 Turn left at Five Corners, past the island in the road.

5.9 The paved surface becomes a dirt road as you head toward Wasque Point.

6.3 Pass the entrance to Wasque Point Reservation.

This 200-acre reservation, created in 1967, is a popular draw for bird-watchers and fishermen.

6.7 At the gatehouse, bear right to the beach.

You may swim or sunbathe. Rest rooms are available. In early October, look for the hawks that migrate across these waters.

7.6 Retrace your route to the paved section of the road.

8.1 Turn left at Five Corners onto Litchfield Road, a dirt road. Note the speed sign, 25 mph, on your right.

9.0 Bear right at the mini-island and the dirt road.

9.8 Turn left onto Main Street, a paved road that leads to the ferry.

10.5 Take the ferry, enjoying a brief view of Edgartown Light. Disembark and go left onto Dock Street.

10.6 Turn right onto Mayhew Lane.

In 1642 Thomas Mayhew founded the oldest island town, incorporated as Edgartown in 1671.

10.7 Turn right onto North Water Street. Turn left immediately onto Winter Street.

On your left, admire St. Andrew's Church.

10.9 Turn left at the stop sign on Pease Point Way.

11.0 At the stop sign, turn right onto Upper Main Street.

11.2 Return to Memorial Park, where your tour began.

Bicycle Repair Services

Cycleworks, 105 State Road, Vineyard Haven, MA 508-693-6966

Wheel Happy, 8 South Water Street, Edgartown, MA 508-627-5928

Wheel Happy II, Beach Road, Edgartown, MA 508-627-3881

Other Bicycle Shops

DeBettencourt's Bike, Circuit Ave. Ext., Oak Bluffs, MA 508-693-0011

Martha's Bicycle, 4 Lagoon Pond Rd., Tisbury, MA 508-693-6593

Ride On Mopeds & Bikes, Lake Ave., Oak Bluffs, MA 508-693-2076

R. W. Cutler Bike Shop, 1 Main St., Edgartown, MA 508-627-4052

Sun and Fun, Lake Ave., Oak Bluffs, MA 508-693-5457

Vineyard Bike & Moped, Oak Bluffs Ave., Oak Bluffs, MA 508-693-6886

Island Sports, 7 Circuit Avenue, Oak Bluffs, MA 508-696-9311

Let Backcountry Guides Take You There

Our experienced backcountry authors will lead you to the finest trails, parks, and back roads in the following areas:

25 Bicycle Tours Series
25 Bicycle Tours in the Adirondacks
25 Bicycle Tours on Delmarva
25 Bicycle Tours in Savannah and the Carolina
   Low Country
25 Bicycle Tours in Maine
25 Bicycle Tours in Maryland
25 Bicycle Tours in the Twin Cities and Southeastern Minnesota
30 Bicycle Tours in New Jersey
30 Bicycle Tours in the Finger Lakes Region
25 Bicycle Tours in the Hudson Valley
25 Bicycle Tours in Ohio's Western Reserve
25 Bicycle Tours in the Texas Hill Country and
   West Texas
25 Bicycle Tours in Vermont
25 Bicycle Tours in and around Washington, D.C.
30 Bicycle Tours in Wisconsin
25 Mountain Bike Tours in the Adirondacks
25 Mountain Bike Tours in the Hudson Valley
25 Mountain Bike Tours in Massachusetts
25 Mountain Bike Tours in New Jersey
25 Mountain Bike Tours in Vermont
Backroad Bicycling in Connecticut
Backroad Bicycling in Eastern Pennsylvania
The Mountain Biker's Guide to Ski Resorts

Bicycling America's National Parks
   Series
Bicycling America's National Parks: Arizona &
   New Mexico
Bicycling America's National Parks: California
Bicycling America's National Parks: Oregon &
   Washington
Bicycling America's National Parks: Utah &
   Colorado

50 Hikes Series
50 Hikes in the Adirondacks
50 Hikes in Connecticut
50 Hikes in the Maine Mountains
50 Hikes in Coastal and Southern Maine
50 Hikes in Massachusetts
50 Hikes in Maryland
50 Hikes in Michigan
50 Hikes in the White Mountains
50 More Hikes in New Hampshire
50 Hikes in New Jersey
50 Hikes in Central New York
50 Hikes in Western New York
50 Hikes in the Mountains of North Carolina
50 Hikes in Ohio
50 Hikes in Eastern Pennsylvania
50 Hikes in Central Pennsylvania
50 Hikes in Western Pennsylvania
50 Hikes in the Tennessee Mountains
50 Hikes in Vermont
50 Hikes in Northern Virginia

Walks and Rambles Series
Walks and Rambles on Cape Cod and the Islands
Walks and Rambles on the Delmarva Peninsula
Walks and Rambles in the Western
   Hudson Valley
Walks and Rambles on Long Island
Walks and Rambles in Ohio's Western Reserve
Walks and Rambles in Rhode Island
Walks and Rambles in and around St. Louis

We offer many more books on hiking, fly-fishing, travel, nature, and other subjects. Our books are available at bookstores and outdoor stores everywhere. For more information or a free catalog, please call 1-800-245-4151 or write to us at The Countryman Press, P.O. Box 748, Woodstock, Vermont 05091. You can find us on the Internet at www.countrymanpress.com.